Astrology

Finding Yourself And Others Through Horoscopes And The 12 Zodiac Signs For Spiritual Growth, Personality Awareness and Self Discovery

Table of Contents

Introduction 1
Chapter 1: The 12 Zodiac Signs 3
Chapter 2 Relationship Astrology: 66
Chapter 3: Finding Yourself through Your Zodiac and Growing on a Spiritual Level 77
Chapter 4: How You Can Strengthen Your Relationships and Friendships by Reading the Zodiac Signs 84
Chapter 5: Birthday Charts 97
Chapter 6: Astrology and the 12 Cell Salts 99
Chapter 7: Extra Information 108
Conclusion 122
Sources and Websites: 123

© Copyright 2018 - All rights reserved.

It is not legal to reproduce, duplicate, or transmit any part of this document in either electronic means or in printed format. Recording of this publication is strictly prohibited and any storage of this document is not allowed unless with written permission from the publisher except for the use of brief quotations in a book review.

Introduction

Your journey may have started with "What is a horoscope?" and "What is my sign?" Astrology is such an interesting topic that just seems to make sense when we read or listen to the traits that come with our specific star sign. Due to the substantial amount of agreement within the population when compared to their zodiac sign, it comes to the point where Horoscopes are quite certainly real. And it is at this moment we realize and accept that we can actually take advantage of our star signs according to you own self and life and even the friendships or relationships we have with others!

This book provides powerful information and allows you to find personality traits that will guide you down the path towards investigating all that you can find using Astrology.

That horoscope or map that appears as a two dimensional chart showing the position of the planets, Moon, and Sun, at the precise moment of when you were born is just the beginning. A thorough horoscope, also known as a natal chart, astrology chart, or the birth chart, can be thought of like the instructions for the hand you have been dealt in this life.

However, following this does not suggest that your life has already been decided. It is largely up to you to decide what you follow and the changes you make based on what your horoscope can tell you. Even given your freedom of choice, your horoscope reflects the natural inclinations you have, your issues to be faced, any lessons you have to learn, and the problems you may have to solve. It may be used as an abstract formula showing the energies you possess or perhaps obstacles have been tasked with.

This book is about the positives of yours and others star signs and how you can use them to your advantage!

Astrology can provide you with information allowing it to be a popular key towards understanding yourself and those around you, but it probably won't provide concrete, clear, or simple answers to your problems. Using the information in your horoscope might give you understanding and insight into the reasons you behave as you do. If you research the horoscope of the people you deal with on a regular basis, you may have a better understanding of the actions of friends, family, or lovers. This can lead to better acceptance, patience, and tolerance of interactions.

The zodiac and the theory of astrology believe mankind is not only influenced by hereditary factors, life experiences, and their environment, but also by the very solar system at the moment of birth and throughout the course of our lives. The planets are viewed as life-forces and these planetary forces take on different aspects, depending on their zodiacal position and how they relate to each another. By reading the roles of the planets, the elements, the signs, and the houses to create a comprehensive reading, astrology presents a picture of a person and their potential based on a birth chart. When you have the the sun, the moon or a planet in a particular sign, then the qualities of that sign are emphasized in your personality and can become a theme through your life experiences. This theme can depend on the planet and sign in question.

Now it's time to get stuck into finding more about star signs. The following chapters will discuss the role that Astrology and the 12 zodiac signs can play in your life.

Chapter 1: The 12 Zodiac Signs

Everyone has always been in search of a deeper meaning to the reality that he or she lives in, something that provides a reason for why we do what we do and who we are. Astrology is not a religion, but it can offer people some guidelines for the interpretation of our present and our future. This information can show us the reasons behind disagreements or guide our steps forward in making a life-changing decision. Astrology indicates that nothing in life is chance. Everything happening at a time and place has a particular reason.

Babylonia is thought to be the birthplace of astrology. They used astrological charts to predict events. They then introduced their form of astrology to the Greeks in the early 4th century B.C. with such followers as Aristotle and Plato. It became regarded as a science and used by the Roman. In fact, the Romans established the zodiac names that we use today. The word "zodiac" came from the Greek term which means "circle of animals." The twelve lunar cycles and twelve constellations were linked to the seasons, and they were then assigned as identifiers (lion, scorpion, bull, etc.). Those twelve signs were then divided into four groups or "houses." Those houses are aligned with the elements of Air, Water, Fire, and Earth. These elements help to further our understanding of the positive and negative traits of our sign. This is based on Earth's daily rotation. At that time, only five planets were known, but it was believed that each of those planets represented a particular trait and area of life and possessed distinctive powers.

- Water signs: emotional and super-sensitive, highly intuitive and mysterious. These signs are Cancer, Pisces, and Scorpio.

- Fire signs: unpredictable, passionate, energetic, can get angry quickly but luckily, can forgive quickly, smart, creative, and idealistic. Come with loads of energy, they are strong and inspire others. These signs are Aries, Leo, and Sagittarius.

- Earth signs: realistic and conservative, but underneath, emotional. Connected to reality, practical, stable, and very loyal. These signs are Capricorn, Taurus, and Virgo.

- Air signs: thinkers, smart, communicative, analytical, and rational. Like giving people advice. Can sometimes be very superficial. These signs are Aquarius, Gemini, and Libra.

There are twelve (12) zodiac signs and each sign is represented by its own glyph, constellation, planet, gemstone, color, the day of the week, and more. Each sign has its own set of traits such as weaknesses, strengths and temperament. For centuries, people have been using this information to plot future choices, pick lovers, and to see what tomorrow will bring.

ARIES – March 20 through April 19			♈ Aries
Symbol:	The Ram	**Quality**	Cardinal
Day of the Week:	Tuesday	**Ruling Planet:**	Mars
Body Part:	head and face	**Secret Desire:**	To be number one
Gemstone:	Diamond	**Color:**	red
Best Compatibility – Overall:	Libra and Leo	**Best Compatibility – Romantic:**	Aquarius, Gemini, Leo, Sagittarius
What they like:	competitive games, new clothes, road trips, debating, expressing themselves with great verbal displays and through physical feats		
What they dislike:	losing, sharing their toys, being ignored, cramped spaces, the word "no"		

Element:	Fire: One of 3 Fire Signs. Since it is the first Fire Sign, many Aries people are trailblazers and trendsetters. Known as "The Spark" – since the Cardinal quality is starting new things and a Fire Sign that spreads energy quite fast. Avoidant personality, always off to new things.
Ruling Planet:	Mars, a warrior planet with a masculine force representing aggression, instincts, and power, can be a source of life-force energy. The negative expression can show up as tactless, argumentative, insensitive, aggressive or confrontational. By being governed by Mars, Aries can be prone to anger but are also daring, highly energetic, impulsive, adventurous, and courageous. Since prone to anger, Aries can have a quick temper that is quick to explode.
Symbol:	The ram is based on the flying ram that provided the Golden Fleece in the mythological story of Jason and the Argonauts. In Greek mythology, Aries was associated with the Amon-Ra, who was depicted as a man with a ram's head. The word "aries" is also the Latin for ram. The glyph is to represent the curving horns of the ram which shows the determination and unceasing energy of this sign.

Aries (cont.)

Personality & Outlook:	Aries have lots of energy and confidence. With their "can-do" attitude, they like new experiences and love to be number one. They can seem selfish or overly focused on themselves, and family and friends may have to remind them to share if their sense of entitlement gets out of control. They may seem abrasive, but will never back down from a challenge. Typically, Aries excel at anything involving competition and feels more alive when leading others and being in control. They can be impatient with those that are in a leadership position whom they feel are not their equal, because they do not like being told what to do by people who are less talented. Since Aries has lots of energy, they are great workers. Their motto can be "Live hard, love hard, work hard," but they can develop tunnel vision about a project which can sometimes make them seem self-centered. If an Aries doesn't get the pat on the back for their accomplishments, it can cause them to become rude and sarcastic. They dislike delays or inactivity. The presence of Aries typically marks the beginning of something stormy and high-energy.

Love/Relationship:	Aries need to take the initiative when it comes to romance. During the early stage of a romance, they will show their feelings before thinking things through completely. They may show their partner lots of attention and affection, even if what they receive is neutral/negative. Aries can be passionate and energetic and enjoys adventures. They may not have sufficient patience to focus on a partner as they have the need for excitement every day.
Money/Job:	A natural born leader, Aries likes issuing orders than receiving them. Their energy and quick mind usually mean that they walk one step ahead of everyone around them. When facing a challenge, they can quickly measure the situation and prepare a solution. They are not intimidated by competition. In fact, it encourages them to perform even better. Aries like to live in the present, so they tend not to focus on the future, which means they can sometimes make mistakes with regards to money decisions. But they will balance their earnings with what they have spent as they always seem to find a way to earn money.
Family/Friends:	Aries are typically tolerant and respectful to those who don't agree with their own. They will feel the most satisfied with a wide range of friends with different views. Honesty and directness are the best way to deal with an Aries.

Aries (cont.)	
Possible Descriptors:	pioneering, confident, dynamic, selfish, foolhardy, enthusiastic, confident, quick-witted, impatient, honest, adventurous, energetic, daredevil, courageous, quick-tempered, impulsive, courageous, determined, confident, passionate, optimistic, moody, impatient, aggressive
Famous Aries:	Lady Gaga, Celine Dion, Aretha Franklin, Keira Knightley, Victoria Beckham, Al Gore, Heath Ledger, Rosie O'Donnell, Gloria Steinheim, Emma Watson, Kourtney Kardashian, Pharrell Williams; Tommy Hilfiger, Maya Angelou, Robert Downey, Jr., Thomas Jefferson
Lucky Numbers:	1, 8, 17

TAURUS - April 20 through May 20

Symbol:	The Bull	Quality	Fixed
Day of the Week:	Friday, Monday	Ruling Planet:	Venus
Body Part:	neck, throat, jaw	Secret Desire:	To own the best of everything
Gemstone:	Emerald	Color:	green, pink
Best Compatibility – Overall:	Scorpio, Cancer	Best Compatibility – Romantic:	Cancer, Virgo, Capricorn, Pisces
What they like:	cooking, photography, gardening, mountains, great music, satin sheets, gourmet food, high-quality clothes, working with hands		
What they dislike:	being rushed, wasting money, dirty things, hotels, mornings, sudden changes, complications, insecurity, synthetic fabrics		
Element:	Earth: known as "The Stone," it relies on its Fixed quality of stability and the Earth element stay consistent. Some may see them as stubborn.		
Ruling Planet:	Venus is the planet of love, luxury and beauty, pleasure, romance, love, femininity, and art		
Symbol:	The glyph depicts the head of the bull with horns. The bull shows the stubbornness, security, and slow/stead habits of this sign.		

Personality & Outlook:	They are typically grounded, unless a hot-button issue has them passionate and heated up. Taurus loves the arts, luxury, and nature. Since Taurus is an Earth Sign, they enjoy nature, but since they like luxury, they will not be roughing it. As they like luxury, they can sometimes be seen as materialistic. Relaxed and peaceful, they are slow to anger, but once engaged, it can be explosive. Taurus enjoys sensual pleasures but look for stability in their lives. Not in a hurry, Taurus is slow to make decisions and may take a long time to commit. But once they do commit, they take it seriously. The way for them to learn is through experience. A Taurus will almost always finish what they have started; usually making a well-informed, correct decision. However, they can be stubborn, which means they might be difficult to get along with, especially in a group project if they are not the leader. Can sometimes be unable to let feelings go. The chief qualities of a Taurus are perseverance and patience.

Taurus (cont.):	
Love/Relationship:	Taurus is the Zodiac's most possessive sign. Male Taurus tends to marry for life and remain dedicated companions, parents, and lovers. Female Taurus is fully committed to a relationship and will be stubborn and slow to leave. But, when/if they feel acutely unappreciated for long enough, they will leave.
Money/Job:	Taurus loves money and will work hard to earn it. As they are reliable, hardworking, patient, and thorough, they will stick firmly to what they are working on. Stability is the key. The materials, pleasures, and rewards they earn can provide their sense of value. Their finances are typically organized and paid on time, saving is part of the plan. As they make money easily, they are suited in careers such as banking, economists, financial advisors, political leaders, art, cooking, and agriculture.

Family/Friends:	Taurus is loyal and always willing to lend a hand. However, they must build trust before any friendship can deepen. Some maintain friendships from childhood their entire life. Once they have established a connection, they will do whatever is necessary to nurture the relationship. Home and family are very important, and they love kids and respects family routines. Taurus loves to laugh and spend time with family and will enjoy hosting house parties and cooking for a room full of people. Taurus collects things, invisible and visible, and sometimes even people. This Earth Sign is known to hold resentment for a long time.
Possible Descriptors:	reliable, possessive, loving, patient, inflexible, persistent, determined, resentful, placid, warm-hearted, self-indulgent, greedy, materialistic, stubborn, stable, conservative, disciplined, loyal, honest, dependable, strong-willed, grounded, realistic
Famous Taurus:	Adele, Al Pacino, David Beckham, Stevie Wonder, Cher, Chris Brown, Channing Tatum, Dwayne Johnson, Megan Fox, George Clooney, Tina Fey, William Shakespeare, James Monroe, Ulysses Grant, Harry Truman
Lucky Numbers:	2, 6, 9, 12, 24

GEMINI – May 21 through June 20   ♊
Gemini

Symbol:	Twins	Quality	Mutable
Day of the Week:	Wednesday	Ruling Planet:	Mercury
Body Part:	shoulders, arms, hands	Secret Desire:	To have all the answers.
Gemstone:	pearl or moonstone	Color:	light-green, yellow
Best Compatibility – Overall:	Sagittarius, Aquarius	Best Compatibility – Romantic:	Aries, Leo, Libra, Aquarius, Sagittarius
What they like:	comedy clubs, cell phones, guitars, fast cars, books, obscure music, trendy clothes		
What they dislike:	Small-minded people, repetition, being confined, dress codes, being alone, silence, authority figures, routines, and nature.		
Element:	Air (first air element of the zodiac). Gemini exhibits great creative synergy, connecting people to each other. Air Sign which can sometimes be known as "The Cool Breeze." Embodying the Mutable quality inherent in a refreshing shift of consciousness, this kind of insight is indicative of the Air element. Although, some believe people that this Air Sign is "all flash and no substance." Air element – all aspects of the mind are connected.		
Quality:	Mutable: As a mutable sign, they know that all things must change, and they are prepared for that eventuality. They can adapt to change rather easily since they are comfortable with it. A plan can be brought to life by a Cardinal sign, then built by a fixed sign, and then		

	polished and perfected by a mutable sign.
Ruling Planet:	Mercury: represents intellect, logic, perception, thinking, and communication. Mercury represents communication, movement, and writing. With the connection to Mercury, Geminis are great communicators, debaters, and intellectuals. Because they are intellectual and multi-taskers, they find it hard to focus on a task for longer periods of time.
Symbol:	Twins or the Roman numeral II is used as a representation to show the duality of this Sign. The twins also show creativity, communication, and resourcefulness which are vital to this Air Sign.

Personality & Outlook	As Gemini is ruled by the dual sign of twins, their energy circulates in a frenzied, quick way. They enjoy witty wordplay and dynamic dialogue, an intellectual meeting of the mind, and a kindred spirit. With a fondness for chatting, they may develop a weakness for gossip and embellishment. Gemini can inspire a roller-coaster ride. They like fast cars, funky new gadgets, trend-setting clothes, games and puzzles; and may seem like they have multiple personalities. Rarely do they like to do anything all alone. Communication is a key element, so they are great at parties, because they can find almost anything to talk about. Led by curiosity, they are adventurous by nature and engage in travel as often as they can afford. People are drawn to them because of their airy and light sparkle. Geminis will crave intellectual stimulation and will push themselves mentally, physically, and spiritually. This means that they end up knowing a little bit about a lot of things. But, they can also be sharp-tongued, selfish, and inconsiderate, thinking only of their own wants. They can also be very superficial with their knowledge, displaying it only for show. They love vibrant colors. Generally optimistic, they despise boredom and have a great sense of humor. A Gemini will enjoy being the center of attention. If they perceive a situation does not seem to be in their favor, they will leave it (career, marriage, relationship, friendship).

	Male Gemini will change jobs often, while females will leave relationships because they are bored. They can have a tendency to suddenly get serious, thoughtful or restless. Since it is represented by twins, some Gemini feels as if their other half is missing. This leads them to seek new friends, mentors, colleagues, loves, and other people to interact with.
Love/Relationship:	May date and flirt a lot before they find a match for their intellect and energy. Since they need passion, variety, and excitement, when they pick, it will be a person who combines lover, friend, and someone to talk to. Geminis will be faithful and determined to treasure their love interest. Some important aspects of the relationship will be excitement, communication, physical contact, and passion. The biggest challenge for a Gemini is to find an emotion and relationship that lasts and avoid any superficial bond that can be disappointing. They have a different perspective on life, one of movement, but are rarely certain of their own direction.

	Gemini (cont.)
Money/Job:	Any suitable job must challenge their minds. Geminis make excellent writers, artists, inventors, journalists, designers, speakers, traders, lawyers, orators, entrepreneurs, or preachers. Inventive, skillful, and smart, they have the need for a dynamic working environment that can provide lots of social contacts. It is important that the workplace not keep them trapped in a routine. Most Geminis do not focus on where the money comes from or how to earn it.
Family/Friends:	Geminis love to spend time with family and friends, especially the younger members. As they love to chat, they will have an abundance of social contacts. In order to stay engaged with family/friends, they will need to be communicated with regularly. The family is very important to a Gemini. The responsibilities of maintaining a family may be a challenge for them, but they are great at multi-tasking, so will use these skills as a parent.
Possible Descriptors:	versatile, youthful, adaptable, nervous, tense, communicative, witty, smart, superficial, inconsistent, eloquent, chatty, lively, cunning, inquisitive, anxious, fascinating, original, charming, resourceful, wise, and adventurous, selfish, sharp-tongued, inconsiderate
Famous Gemini:	Angelina Jolie, Kanye West, Prince, Johnny Depp, Donald Trump, Tupac Shakur, Macklemore, Kendrick Lamar, Iggy Azalea, Blake Shelton, Kate Upton, Amy Schumer, John F. Kennedy, George

	Bush, Harriet Beecher Stowe, George Orwell,
Lucky Numbers:	5, 7, 14, 23

CANCER – June 21 through July 22

Symbol:	Crab	**Quality**	Cardinal
Day of the Week:	Monday, Thursday	**Ruling Planet:**	Moon
Body Part:	Stomach, chest	**Secret Desire:**	To take care of friends and family
Gemstone:	Ruby	**Color:**	white
Best Compatibility – Overall:	Capricorn, Taurus	**Best Compatibility – Romantic:**	Taurus, Virgo, Pisces, Capricorn
What they like:	working with kids, gourmet meals, helping loved ones, relaxing near or in water, museum/art galleries, intramural sports, home-based hobbies, hosting parties.		
What they dislike:	playing with art supplies, tacky clothes, puttering in the kitchen, being rushed, paying full price, shopping for antiques, listening to live music, public speaking, frozen dinners.		
Element:	Water sign sometimes known as "The Rain." The first water sign, Cancer is a fluid sign that gets the creativity and emotions flowing. This makes those under this Water Sign excellent caretaker, as they frequently make sure everyone around them is contented and happy. This can give them a deep need to spend time with family. As a water sign, it means they have a deep and mysterious side.		
Quality:	Cardinal signs are characterized by starting things. They are visionaries and trailblazers. They may get lost during their journey, but what they find along the way will change		

	things for the better. But, once they start something new, they may not stay around long enough to see it finished.
Ruling Planet:	Moon: represents moods, the feminine, emotions, intuition, mothers, and children. It affects our moods more than any other planet. Rules the inner self, bringing to life the deepest desires of the soul and cravings of our emotions. Since the Moon governs Cancer, they tend to be curious about habits and traditions, and they can be changeable and adaptive. However, they also need a lot of reassurance, can be demanding and are very timid.
Symbol:	The glyph represents either a crab with sideways claws or a woman's breasts, as this sign represents mothers and women. This shows the nurturing, feminine qualities of this Water Sign, and that Cancer is the caretaker of the zodiac rooting for the family, children, and home.

	Cancer (cont.)
Personality & Outlook:	Cancer will cling to a job for security and beloved family members/pets. It is important for them to set up a cozy and safe space. For them, change can be threatening. The essence of the energy of Cancer is sensitivity, feminity, domesticity, maternal instincts, compassion, romance, caretaking, and creativity. The negative energy of a Cancer leans to gossip, being hypersensitive, cliques, and being overly competitive. Their intuitions and emotions can overshadow logic and intellect. They are guided by their emotion and heart. Since they are guided by the moon, they may have emotional patterns that are beyond their control. They may play it too safe and can end up feeling smothered, which can then devolve into co-dependence or coddling. Cancers are homebodies at heart, especially female ones, and can be passionate foodies who love to eat and cook. As homebodies, they love house parties and are great with pets and kids, so they make excellent parents and caretakers. They may sometimes make a step like a crab – sideways – in order to face a fight or obtain a goal. They tend to grasp onto what makes them happy and refuse let go. Those under the sign of Cancer need to be needed and want to know they matter. And if their needs are not met, they may turn moody, shy, reserved, clingy, insecure, or brooding. They also have an offbeat sense of

	humor. They are good listeners, dependable and reliable. They are deeply intuitive and sentimental and can be challenging to get to know.
Love/Relationship:	The thing that is most important for them are their feelings, as emotions are very important to Cancer. They wear their heart on their sleeves and are gentle and caring. They prefer a person who can understand them, even when they are not talking. Their affection for anyone who is flaky, superficial or unreliable will be fleeting. They enjoy being in a committed relationship so they can have a sense of security. They may change their beliefs and opinions to match those that they love because that love is important. When in a relationship with Cancer, never take for granted any understanding, love or compassion they show you.
Money/Job:	A Cancer will roll up their sleeves to get the job done and get it done right. Typically, they work better alone than in a group. Loyal to their employers. Good career choices: gardener, nurse, housekeeper, decorator, politician.

	Cancer (cont.)
Family/Friends:	Since a Cancer is dedicated to their family, they can make unhealthy choices just to keep a healthy image of a family in place. This could lead them to choosing partners who repeat a cycle of abuse or bad behavior. Cancers communicate easily. Since this is a Sign of family, they enjoy having fun at the comfort of their homes in a more familiar atmosphere and will diligently preserve family memories. They are intuitive and compassionate. When they are content with their personal lives, they can be a parent that is very caring and has deep bond with their children.
Possible Descriptors:	loving, moody, emotional, imaginative, touchy, clingy, sensitive, intuitive, shrewd, cautious, protective, sympathetic, compassionate, romantic, maternal, hypersensitive, co-dependent, shy, reserved, insecure, brooding, sentimental
Famous Cancers:	Meryl Streep, Tom Cruise, Ariana Grande, Selena Gomez, Khloe Kardashian, Kourtney Kardashian, Vin Diesel, Robin Williams, Lindsay Lohan, Courtney Love, Pamela Anderson, O.J. Simpson, Gerald Ford, George W. Bush, Nathaniel Hawthorn, Ernest Hemingway, Emily Bronte, Vera Wang,
Lucky Numbers:	2, 3, 15, 20

LEO – July 23 through August 23

Symbol:	lion	Quality	Fixed
Day of the Week:	Sunday	Ruling Planet:	Sun
Body Part:	heart, upper back, spine	Secret Desire:	To rule the world.
Gemstone:	Peridot	Color:	gold, yellow-orange
Best Compatibility – Overall:	Aquarius, Gemini	Best Compatibility – Romantic:	Aries, Gemini, Libra, Sagittarius
What they like:	bright colors, theater, fun with friends, expensive things, being admired, holidays		
What they dislike:	being ignored, not being treated as an important person, facing difficult reality		
Element:	Fire sign sometimes known as "The Bonfire." Fire combined with the fixed nature edifies all around those and provides warmth. The second fire sign of the zodiac, Leo turns up the heat and are typically natural born leaders and magnetic performers.		
Quality:	Fixed sign; able to take the imaginative idea from a Cardinal sign and bring it to life into something real. Leo is trustworthy individuals who like a clear and concrete "to do" list.		
Ruling Planet:	Sun: representing life, vitality, ego, creativity, and expression. Typically, the sun constitutes a masculine ego and the life force.		
Symbol:	The glyph depicts a lion with a mane and both sides of a heart. A lion represents boldness, passion, drama, and playful qualities of this sign.		

Personality & Outlook:	Leos are in charge, regal, and proud. They like relaxation, comfort, and warmth. Leo will focus on the big picture, not the small details or fine print. Typically, they will have no patience for boring, complicated, or overly-involved. As natural leaders, they don't do well when they have to take orders. Love is most important to Leos. To be loved and have someone to love is their primary motivation. Their feelings will be hurt if they go unrecognized for an accomplishment. People will be drawn to them because of their warmth and energy. Leos tend to be honest, decent, and do the right thing. Appreciate luxury, materials goods, and organization but have a weakness for extravagance. With a great sense of self-worth, they can sometimes cross over into arrogance. They may end up smothering their mates and friends, which may cause some people to leave them. They will find this devastating, since Leo is all about family and community. Since they are generous and loyal, Leos will have a lot of friends. With self-confidence, they are good at leading a group toward a common goal. In love with life and warmhearted with a healthy sense of humor, Leos are good at taking the initiative necessary to resolve complicated situations. They are comfortable with asking for what they

	Leo (cont.)
Personality & Outlook (cont.)	need, but can unconsciously neglect what those around them need because they are in their own pursuits and search for self-awareness. Leos love attention and must have it at all costs. They can be materialistic and high maintenance.
Love/Relationship:	Sincere and passionate, Leos demonstrate their feelings with ease. They are loyal, fun, respectful, and generous. Will typically take on the role of the leader in any relationship. But this may end up being aggravating to their partner if they impose their will too frequently and with a heavy hand. A Leo needs a partner who is reasonable, self-aware, reasonable, and can match their level of intelligence.
Money/Job:	Highly energetic, ambitious, and creative, Leos like to be busy. Once they are dedicated to a job or career, they will work hard and do it just right. The best position is for them to hold is for them to be their own bosses or manage others with little supervision. Leos like jobs that allow them to express artistic talent. Like to be surrounded by cutting-edge gadgets and money comes easily to them, but they spend it less responsibly. Generous at heart, they may end up getting taken advantage of by friend or acquaintance by giving out money. They can excel and use their talents to shine like their governing Sun in the entertainment field.
Family/Friends:	They are a loyal friend, generous, and faithful. Leos are born with the need to

	help others and are good at doing so since they are strong and reliable. They do not like to be alone, since they seem to get their self-esteem from their interactions with family and friends. They are tuned into their feelings, emotions, and mindset more than others. Family may not be their first priority but will do whatever they can to protect their loved ones.
Possible Descriptors:	generous, faithful, loving, bossy, dogmatic, expansive, creative, interfering, pompous, patronizing, warm-hearted, enthusiastic, broad-minded, regal, proud, honest, arrogant, passionate, energetic, intelligent
Famous Leo:	Mila Kunis, Madonna, Daniel Radcliffe, Chris Hemsworth, Halle Berry, Charlize Theron, J.K. Rowling, Robert DeNiro, Anna Kendrick, Tom Brady, Arnold Schwarzenegger, Whitney Houston, Jennifer Lawrence, Bill Clinton, Coco Chanel, Jennifer Lopez, Barack Obama
Lucky Numbers:	1, 3, 10, 19

VIRGO August 23 through September 23

Symbol:	Maiden	**Quality**	Mutable
Day of the Week:	Wednesday	**Ruling Planet:**	Mercury
Body Part:	stomach, waist, digestive system	**Secret Desire:**	To be a hero
Gemstone:	Sapphire	**Color:**	grey, beige, pale yellow
Best Compatibility – Overall:	Pisces, Cancer	**Best Compatibility – Romantic:**	Taurus, Cancer, Scorpio, Capricorn, Pisces
What they like:	long showers with deeply scented soaps, outdoor concerts, laptops, magazines, trivia games, childhood friends		
What they dislike:	spicy food, vulgar people, laziness, leaving home		
Element:	This Earth sign is sometimes known as "The Landslide." They make an impact in the material world. As the second Earth sign, Virgo builds a plan around the foundation that Taurus put in place. Virgo's energy motivates us to try new ways to do old projects. This energy can also get people stuck in "what if" mode and make them anxious or nervous.		
Quality:	Mutable sign: Virgos know that all things must change and must prepare everyone for that eventuality. They can adapt to new conditions since they are comfortable with change.		
Ruling	Mercury: representing intellect, logic,		

Planet:	perception, thinking and communication, the ability to multi-task and check off the never-ended activity list. Roman god Mercury, the winged messenger, who carried out the tasks of the gods.
Symbol:	The glyph is designed to depict either a maiden carrying a shaft of wheat, intestines or virginity. The use of the maiden shows the qualities of innocence and serving for this sign.
Personality & Outlook:	Virgos are usually cool, calm, and mild-mannered on the surface, but underneath there is lots of activity. They are usually thinking, calculating, and assessing the situation. Gardening is one of their favorite hobbies, since they are very nurturing and love to grow things. This is perfect for them as they enjoy alone time as well. Since they tend to be detail-oriented, Virgos make excellent strategists. However, they can get overburdened because they struggle to say "no" to those asking for help. This can also cause them to be taken advantage by those that are aware of this. Kind, good-natured, patient, they love to laugh and can be sympathetic listeners. Male Virgos are very committed to a relation, almost never walking away from it, unless they are betrayed.

	Virgo (cont.)
Personality & Outlook (cont.):	Female Virgos are very good at parenting, being dedicated mothers, and may even mother kids that aren't theirs. This includes playing nursemaid as they are very aware of health matters (however, this can sometimes lead them to be hypochondriacs). But, they can also be critical or judgmental about anyone they feel is not living up to their potential. They are very opinionated, and they will express that opinion even to those that didn't ask to hear it. Although careful, they can also be a little blunt in delivering their message which may come across a little sharp. Although they pay attention, they worry that they might miss a detail that will change a situation they cannot remedy. This can cause them to get stuck in a loop that can make them critical of themselves and others. This may also cause them to become a perfectionist. In this regard, they love organization, order, cleanliness, and dedication. They also have a well-developed sense of speech and writing (communication). However, Virgos can be shy and only open up to people they trust. They are also very sensual when they open up in love and romance.
Love/Relationship:	Virgos need to feel safe before they expose themselves and be vulnerable. They will pursue a potential partner so the romance can provide the love and self-worth they lack. A stable, long-term relationship is preferred over multiple

	one-night stands. Trust needs to be built slowly and patiently, and they should be nurtured and cared for. Virgos are attracted to intelligence.
Money/Job:	Their approach allows them to excel at a number of careers, especially those requiring organization skills, paperwork, and problem-solving. Virgos are hard-working, practical, and analytical. They have a great eye for details and are very attuned to matters of health. They are very good in service industry and excel in jobs including: nurses, critics, doctors, writers, journalists, teachers, typists, caregivers, counselors, and psychologists. Typically, Virgos are very good at saving money and will put something away for a rainy day. Their preference is for a practical and economical solution. However, sometimes this can come across as cheap and stingy.

	Virgo (cont.)
Family/Friends:	They know how to solve problems and this makes them a good person to go to for advice. Virgos will nurture the family and friends that surround them. To become closer and more intimate with a Virgo, do something good for someone you know or your community. Good deeds are a way to their inner circle. Tradition is important, and they are very proud of their heritage and ancestry and dedicated to their family. Will be especially attentive to elderly and sick grandparents, aunts, uncles, and other family members.
Possible Descriptors:	diligent, intelligent, cool, patient, modest, overcritical, fussy, meticulous, practical, analytical, shy, reliable, worrier, harsh, perfectionist, conservative, calm, calculating, kind, critical, judgmental
Famous Virgos:	Beyoncé, Michael Jackson, Bernie Sanders, Cameron Diaz, Paul Walker, Kobe Bryant, Jimmy Fallon, Flo Rida, Adam Sandler, Pink, Sean Connery, Amy Poehler, Lyndon B. Johnson, Mary Shelley, Leo Tolstoy, Agatha Christie, Stephen King
Lucky Numbers:	5, 14, 15, 23, 32

LIBRA September 23 through October 23

Symbol:	Scales	**Quality**	Cardinal
Day of the Week:	Friday	**Ruling Planet:**	Venus
Body Part:	lower back, butt	**Secret Desire:**	To be loved and love in return
Gemstone:	Opal	**Color:**	pink, green
Best Compatibility – Overall:	Aries, Sagittarius	**Best Compatibility – Romantic:**	Aquarius, Gemini, Leo, Sagittarius
What they like:	harmony, gentleness, sharing with others, the outdoors (outdoor concerts prime), poetry, good books, lively debates, expensive jewelry, rich food, designer clothes		
What they dislike:	violence, injustice, loudmouths, conformity, unhappy people, dull people, practical people, bullies, pressure to make a decision and hearing "maybe".		
Element:	Cardinal Air sign sometimes known as "Exhaling," Libras put new energy out into the world. Some may see people with this sign as "all talk and no action." However, as the second air sign, it builds on Gemini's expansive gusts of air, and Libra then shapes them into winds of grace, good manners, and charm. This means, you may change without even knowing you are doing so. Libra inspires a successful relationship through compromise which may include inspiring teamwork.		

Quality:	Cardinal sign: Libra begins the Fall season so it is considered a leader and is typically "idea" people. Those under this sign are trendsetters and prize originality and like to be first.
Ruling Planet:	Venus: The planet represents femininity, pleasure, romance, love, luxury, beauty and art. Venus, the goddess of love, adds charm and enhances everything she touches such as beauty, your personality, fashion, food, art, etc.
Symbol:	This is the only sign that is represented by an object, not a living thing. The glyph represents the scales, symbolizing harmony and balance. This is displayed by the fairness and equality of those under this sign.
Personality & Outlook:	Libras need to remain aware and keep balance in family, work, recreational, health, and spirit. As they need to weigh all the options before making a decision, they can seem indecisive. What makes them unhappy is to see those around them unhappy, since they do not like to see others unhappy. Peace and harmony are the keys to happiness for a Libra. However, they do have such a strong sense of fair play

Libra (cont.)	
Personality & Outlook (cont.)	that if they think they (or others) are being treated unfairly, this may lead to conflict. A person under this sign might benefit from practicing meditation, in order to provide balance in their life, but most will at least enjoy some type of physical exercise that involves a mental component. They don't necessarily like to be the leader, but do want to ensure that their voices are heard. Although they like justice, equality and balance, they can carry a grudge. They will try to avoid confrontations but hate being alone, the partnership is important to them. Possess a strong intellect and a keen mind. Tend to be fond of expensive, material things and will dress well. Kind and considerate, romance, love, and marriage are a must for Libra. They are perhaps the most popular of the signs of the Zodiac and make the best friends.

Love/Relationship:	Finding a life partner will probably be one of the main priorities in Libra's life, and they should pick someone who encourages the expression of their own opinions. For a truly happy relationship, their partner should enhance the partnership with travel, music, art, and expensive gifts. Libra may be best satisfied by a partner who can set clear boundaries, thereby protecting them but without endangering their pride. Once they have that romantic relationship, the primary goal will be to maintain peace and harmony. Libra is the sign of marriage, so most people under this sign will go the traditional route. Even though they are flexible as an Air Sign, they will still gravitate to tradition and their journey will eventually lead to an officiant and bouquet. Part of the inspiration for this may be to create a certain image for the outer world. Since Libra is connected to Scorpio, they are sexual and seek a meaningful relationship where a complete surrender of body and soul can occur. Libra corresponds to the Seventh House (the Marriage House) which deals with the law, marriage and divorce, partnerships, and alliances. No other sign of the Zodiac requires romance and marriage like the Libra.

	Libra (cont.)
Money/Job:	Whatever career path they seek, Libras will not typically become a workaholic as they are more focused on the balance in their life. Balancing family, private time, work, and spouse is the key to their happy life. They will be loved if they become a leader, but do not necessarily have a penchant for this as they struggle with decision making and may lack the initiative to organize their employees. If they do rise to a position of power, they will work very hard to deserve those privileges that go with the position. Since they search for equality, truth and justice, they are good judicial officers, lawyers, diplomats and their artistic side can make them good composers or designers. The money is usually under control, but that may be a fluke because they can't decide what to indulge their finances in. They do like expensive material things. But rarely do they left their spending get the better of them and only occasionally indulge in fine clothes or expensive jewelry.

Family/Friends:	Highly social, Libras put their friends in the limelight, but can sometimes choose friends that allow them to feel superior. Their friends may struggle with their indecisive nature when planning activities. But, if they are not the initiator of the friendship, they will participate whole-heartedly. Since they are tactful and can remain calm, they often mediate between themselves and others and also between other friends who are in conflict. Libras can be self-sacrificing for the good of the family, but will also use guilt as a weapon against them. May agree with stronger family members simply to keep peace and harmony in the house. They may embrace parenting as a way to share their knowledge and views, but only if they are secure with their own inner sense of power.
Possible Descriptors:	Charming, cooperative, diplomatic, gracious, fair-minded, social, indecisive, peaceful, fair, tactful, honest, open-minded, deceitful/lying, vain, frivolous, superficial, vacillating, conservative, refined, tactful, honest, open-minded, loyal, faithful, sociable, urbane, idealistic, diplomatic, indecisive
Famous Libra:	Bruno Mars, Scott Fitzgerald, John Lennon, Simon Cowell, Snoop Dogg, Eminem, F. Ralph Lauren, Kim Kardashian, Zac Efron, Gwen Stefani, Mahatma Gandhi, Vladimir Putin, Jimmy Carter, Dwight D. Eisenhower, Donna Karan
Lucky Numbers:	4, 6, 13, 15, 24

SCORPIO-October 23 through November 22

Scorpio

Symbol:	Scorpion	Quality	Fixed
Day of the Week:	Tuesday	Ruling Planet:	Pluto
Body Part:	crotch, reproductive organs	Secret Desire:	To have complete and total control
Gemstone:	Topaz or citrine	Color:	scarlet, red, rust
Best Compatibility – Overall:	Taurus, Cancer	Best Compatibility – Romantic:	Cancer, Virgo, Capricorn, Pisces
What they like:		truth, facts, being right, teasing, longtime friends, spicy food, danger, probing questions, underground music, unique items, organic food
What they dislike:		revealing secrets, dishonesty, passive people, simple-minded people, personal questions, insincere flattery, living at someone else's house
Element:		Fixed Water Sign, which can be called "Ice." The Cancer's tides are directed by the second water sign into forceful torrents of energy. It is connected more closely to the darker side of life and the unexamined areas. This allows them to see beneath the surface into spirituality. They can sometimes be obsessed about a lover or project, displaying insecurity or jealousy.
Quality:		Fixed sign Scorpio is a stabilizer, taking the creativity of Cardinal signs and starting to build the foundation of a plan. The Fixed quality shows the nature of the Water.

Ruling Planet:	Pluto: the Underworld's Greek god and all things occult. Since Scorpio also has a lesser ruler in Mars (the Greek god of War) since Pluto was just found in the 1930s. Pluto represents power, healing, transformation, obsession, alchemy, and life and death (creation/destruction). Mars represents war, energy, anger, initiative, adventure, courage, and impulse.
Symbol:	The glyph represents a scorpion with the pointy tail. Scorpion was used to represent intensity, depth, and obsessiveness.
Personality & Outlook:	Scorpios can crave time alone and will be annoyed if they don't get it. They are great secret keepers and feel their emotions more intensely than other signs, typically becoming self-aware at an earlier age. This makes emotions very important to a Scorpio. They believe in defending those that lack that ability and require being a leader. Scorpios are typically great leaders, since they are resourceful and alert to their surroundings. They excel at problem solving, and this leads them to also be interested in what makes people tick.

Scorpio (cont.)

Personality & Outlook (cont.):	They will research topics and people until they find out the truth. They exert extreme self-control and those around them are expected to do so as well. Scorpio invented the word "vendetta," as they never forgive and forget and will definitely get even. Those under this sign also tend to be suspicious, pessimistic, stubborn, and occasionally even paranoid. However, they are also known for their calm and cool behavior. Scorpio love a good challenge, will thrive from it, and obstacles won't even dissuade them. They love winning.
Love/Relationship:	A sensual sign, intimacy and passion are very important to them. They desire to have honest and smart partners. Once a Scorpio falls in love, they are dedicated and faithful. They prefer to build a relationship slowly until they build trust and respect. Be careful when ending a relationship with a Scorpio and do your best to ensure that it is a mutual and amicable split, as this is the most vengeful sign in the zodiac. A Scorpio ex can be a very bad thing.

Money/Job:	Good at being a leader and management and when they set a goal for the team, company or themselves, they achieve it. The focus and determination they use in approaching a task make them good managers. However, they rarely mix business with friendship, so socializing at work will be at a minimum. Good jobs for a Scorpio are researcher, scientist, sailor, police, detective, physician, psychologist/counselor, and business manager. When it comes to money, they are disciplined enough to stick to a budget. Although they are not afraid of hard work to earn it, they are also not inclined to spend a lot of money.
Family/Friends:	Scorpios look for fairness and honesty when it comes to searching for a friend. Scorpios can make great friends, since they are dedicated and loyal. Smart and quick-witted, they prefer the company of fun-loving people who can keep up. However, if you let them down just once, there is probably no bouncing back from it. When they are hurt, they are very emotional, so it is hard to make them feel better. They are dedicated and they take good care of their family.

	Scorpio (cont.)
Possible Descriptors:	frank, determined, pessimistic, suspicious, courageous, stubborn and paranoid, honest, resourceful, brave, passionate, stubborn, constructive, distrusting, passionate, open, spiritual, affectionate, tender and loving, sensitive, obsessive, sincere, vengeful, persevering, strong-willed, intuitive, perceptive, jealous, secretive, violent, assertive, decisive
Famous Taurus:	Robert Louis Stevenson Sylvia Plath, Theodore Roosevelt, John Adams, Julia Roberts, Ryan Reynolds, Ryan Gosling, Emma Stone, Lorde, Calvin Kline, Puff Daddy, Kendall Jenner, Caitlyn Jenner, Kris Jenner, Bill Gates, Leonardo DiCaprio, Katy Perry, Drake, Hillary Clinton
Lucky Numbers:	8, 11, 18, 22

SAGITTARIUS - November 22 through December 22

Sagittarius

Symbol:	centaur or archer	**Quality**	Mutable
Day of the Week:	Thursday	**Ruling Planet:**	Jupiter
Body Part:	thighs, hips	**Secret Desire:**	To be the one to make the rules
Gemstone:	turquoise or tanzanite	**Color:**	blue
Best Compatibility – Overall:	Gemini, Aries	**Best Compatibility – Romantic:**	Aries, Libra, Leo, Aquarius
What they like:	freedom, traveling, being outside, philosophy, pets, flirting, laughing, karaoke, dares, books, stories that inspire		
What they dislike:	crazy theories, details, people who cling, being constrained, prejudice, boredom, being told "you can't," routine		
Element:	Fire Sign is sometimes known as "The Wildfire." The third and final Fire Sign, Sagittarius combines Aries' trailblazing with Leo's leadership to create an explosion of wisdom and action. Sagittarius pushes us to go after endless possibilities, as they are the eternal optimist.		
Quality:	Mutable: They know that all good things must change and their role is to help others prepare for the change. They will change to adapt to situations.		

	Their mutable quality of unchecked energy shows up as a burst. However, that unchecked burst of energy may quickly burn out, just like a wildfire.
Ruling Planet:	Jupiter: Represents luck, growth, abundance, expansion, higher learning, travel, and religion. Since the planet is the largest in the solar system, those under this sign can also have big personalities. Jupiter was the most widely revered Roman god, leading Sagittarians to want the biggest and the best, sometimes to the point of over-indulgence.
Symbol:	The glyph represents the arrow of the centaur or an archer. The arrow of the glyph points upwards to show optimism and the higher spiritual ideal. This represents the honesty and wisdom of this sign.
Personality & Outlook:	Love discovering new things, travel, the open road, and meeting new people. Will be very unhappy tied to a normal routine, as they will become restless without variety. Highly intelligent, they enjoy learning and will question everything. Big daydreamers, but can get carried away with unrealistic or grandiose plans, and they sometimes lack in follow-through since they become easily sidetracked by new adventures. May focus on the big picture and get bogged down with details. With this daydreaming quality, they may come across as just a "big talker," promising more than they can deliver. But, with their generous, idealistic, and fun sense of humor,

	those around them will quickly forgive this shortcoming.
Sagittarius (cont.)	
Personality & Outlook (cont.):	Give them ample space, as they do not like being confined and will travel with an open mind. This penchant for spirituality and philosophy may inspire them to wander the world in search of the meaning of life. Sagittarius wants to constantly be in touch with the world in order to experience as much as possible. Freedom is priceless to them just so they can explore and travel. Honest and forthright, sometimes to the point of sometimes being tactless, they are open and very broad-minded.
Love/Relationship:	Considered to be the happiest of the signs. Willing to try almost anything, since they are incredibly playful, humorous, open, passionate, and expressive. It might take them a while to get serious and settle down, as they embrace diversity and change. This may cause them to go through a string of partners before finding the one they commit to. However, once truly in love, they are faithful, loyal, and completely dedicated. They do best with partners who are smart, sensitive and expressive.
Money/Job:	If they can envision their goal, they do almost anything to achieve it. They like a position with a changing atmosphere and different tasks. Good jobs: photographer, researcher, salesperson, artist, interviewers, reporter, talk-show host, travel agent, artist, ambassador, importer/exporter. Enjoy making/spending money. Doesn't much

	care where they will earn their money, but feel the need to take risks, even if they appear foolish or impractical. They typically believe that the universe will simply provide them with what they need. They are not good at managing the finances and money, as they are undisciplined and waste a lot of energy.
Family/Friends:	Usually surrounded by friends since they are fun to be with. They love to laugh and enjoy diversity in their circle of friends. Dedicated to family and generous with their time, affection, and help.
Possible Descriptors:	daydreamer, lucky, creative, generous, idealistic, impatient, tactless, curious, energetic, extroverted, enthusiastic, honest, tolerant, restless, outspoken, undisciplined, opportunistic, humorous, playful
Famous Sagittarius:	Brad Pitt, Taylor Swift, Miley Cyrus, Britney Spears, Sia, Winston Churchill, Mark Twain, Jay-Z, Frank Sinatra, Sammy Davis, Jr., Vanessa Hudgens, Scarlett Johannsson, Christina Aguilera, Jake Gyllenhaal, Chrissy Teigen, Emily Dickinson, Manolo Blahnik, Joseph Stalin
Lucky Numbers:	3, 7, 9, 12, 21

CAPRICORN December 22 through January 20

Capricorn

Symbol:	mountain goat	**Quality**	Cardinal
Day of the Week:	Saturday	**Ruling Planet:**	Saturn
Body Part:	skin, bones, knees, teeth	**Secret Desire:**	To have every need taken care of
Gemstone:	Garnet	**Color:**	brown, black
Best Compatibility – Overall:	Taurus, Cancer	**Best Compatibility – Romantic:**	Taurus, Virgo, Scorpio, Pisces
What they like:	music, family, quality craftsmanship, tradition, understated status, goals, titles, exclusive clubs, motorcycles, sports involving running, being in charge		
What they dislike:	a whole host of things at some point throughout their lives, careless mistakes, roaming without a plan, doing things without purpose, quitting, shouting in public		
Element:	Earth Sign sometimes called "The meteor" as they will go independently into new worlds. The Earth elements make Capricorn solid and absolute. The third and final Earth Sign, they combine the foundation of Taurus with Virgo's planning. Capricorns keep the big picture in view and are, therefore, good at strategy, and may inspire them to take on big goals.		

Quality:	Cardinal Sign, the first winter sign, which means they are lead or "idea" people. This means that they like originality and want to be a trendsetter (the first one to use/create something new).
Ruling Planet:	Saturn: represents the structure, restrictions, time, authority, research, discipline, hard work, delay, obstacles, privation, pessimism, and lasting reward after a long struggle, and limitations. Saturn (aka Cronus) was Father Time. Saturn is the planet of repression, so Capricorn may hide a few freaky secrets under their calm exterior.
Symbol:	The glyph represents the goat as a working-class animal and this sign is a working-class sign. Capricorn makes long-term plans, often earning awards and drawing acclaim. In some representations, the goat is combined with a fish's tail to show that imagination and creativity will work in combination with that planning.
Personality & Outlook:	Capricorn is usually goal-oriented and driven to succeed, so they will work hard and put in long hours. As achievement is very important, they tend to be self-disciplined and successful. Take life seriously and are not very tolerant of other people who do not. Very good at making decisions, since they are realistic and logical. Family-oriented, unless their family members are negative or harmful, in which case, they will ensure they keep distance between themselves and family. Dry sense of humor, sarcastic, so they may not be everyone's "cup of tea."

Capricorn (cont.)	
Personality & Outlook (cont.)	To those that don't know them well, they can seem dull or less imaginative since they are focused on the big picture. While on the surface they can come across as lacking in emotion, there is lots of activity running through their minds. May seem to be selfish or stingy and secretive with information, since they guard their hearts closely. Capricorns hate being wrong. Because their focus is on the material world, this can make them seem stiff and stubborn when it comes to changing their perspective when necessary. Can seem to be intolerant as they have a hard time accepting those that vary too much from their own perspective. Serious by nature and traditional, yet with an inner state of independence. Masters of self-control, those under this sign are very good at leading the way. They will learn from their mistakes, but they need to learn to forgive, so as to avoid being stuck in the past and alleviate their pessimistic nature. Capricorns can also be pessimistic and negative, especially if they perceive obstacles in their path.

Love/Relationship:	Although the beginning of a relationship with a Capricorn will be difficult, once you breach the outer defenses and they are in love, they will stay committed for a lifetime. For romance to be effective, it should be demonstrated through action, not just words. However, it still may take years before they open up enough to talk about their feelings. They may seem emotionally or lacking in compassion in dealing with their loved ones. Their partner will be able to rely on them as there will be a lasting bond between them that will accept the constant tendency to grow, change, and evolve. But any partner of Capricorn should not count on them compromising very often.

Capricorn (cont.)

Money/Job:	Very career oriented. Will set very high standards for themselves. Their dedication, honesty, and perseverance will help them to achieve goals. Capricorns value hard work and loyalty the most, and this can offset negative traits of those they work with, even if that has less talent or intelligence. They don't mind putting in the extra hours, are resourceful, and will get the job done. Good with numbers and analysis. Best jobs would involve management, calculations, finance, politician, diplomat, mathematician, and possibly programming. They like tradition, so jobs that involve a lot of paperwork don't bother them (but the paperwork must be orderly and neat). Those under this sign value money and will be good at managing it and saving it. Can be good diplomats and politicians, as they are good at cutting through red tape and seeing the bottom line. Like all Earth signs, Capricorns have great savvy, acumen, and business skills, and are conservative with money and good with finances.

Family/Friends:	Although they are good friends and very loyal, Capricorns will not list a lot of people in their inner circle. Since they guard their hearts closely, it will take time for anyone new to get into their inner circle. They prefer to be around people who aren't nosy and don't ask too many questions. They are open-hearted and will choose friends who can carry on a lively, intelligent conversation, make them feel peaceful, and will be honest with them. Since they feel connected to everything in their past, friends can expect to hear the same stories told repeatedly, to look through old photos and watch family movies. As parents, they can be strict but are usually fair. Capricorns want to be respected for their role as head of the family.
Possible Descriptors:	Persevering, reliable, trustworthy, stable, persistent, patient, ambitious, self-reliant, logical, ambitious, good self-control, determined, diligent, honorable, miserly, sarcastic, pessimistic, unforgiving, realistic, grounded, careful, practical, loyal, prudent, humorous, disciplined, know-it-all, responsible, hard-working, down-to-earth, and charitable,

	Capricorn (cont.)
Famous Capricorn:	David Bowie, Muhammad Ali, Kate Middleton, Martin Luther King, Jr., Michelle Obama, Denzel Washington, Nicolas Cage, Meghan Trainor, Elvis Presley, Pitbull, Liam Hemsworth, Jared Leto, Howard Stern, Betty White, Richard Nixon, Nicolas Sparks, J.R.R. Tolkein, Edgar Allen Poe
Lucky Numbers:	4, 8, 13, 22

AQUARIUS January 20 through February 18

Aquarius

Symbol:	water bearer	**Quality**	Fixed
Day of the Week:	Saturday	**Ruling Planet:**	Uranus
Body Part:	ankles	**Secret Desire:**	To experience total freedom
Gemstone:	Amethyst	**Color:**	light blue or silver
Best Compatibility – Overall:	Leo, Sagittarius	**Best Compatibility – Romantic:**	Aries, Gemini, Libra, Sagittarius
What they like:	teaching, team sports, a cause/mission, computer programming, independent films		
What they dislike:	owing money, feeling isolated, injustice, drama queens		
Element:	An Air Sign sometimes referred to as "The Deep Breath." They instinctively know what thoughts are commonplace and will know what people want simply by being with them. Although, that does not necessarily make Aquarius one of them. The third and final Air Sign, it adds Gemini's gusts with the whirlwind that is Libra to create a gale of humanitarian causes. This makes them visionaries, causing them (and others) to get involved with a new cause, join a new social group, or have a mission in life. People born under a water sign see the world as a place full of possibilities.		

Quality:	Fixed sign – stabilizer who takes the creativity of the Cardinal and starts to build a plan.
Ruling Planet:	Uranus: represents rebellion, revolution, emotional detachment, unpredictable energy, individualism, eccentricity, humanitarianism, fashion, modern science, and inventions. Uranus was the sky god. Some schools believe Aquarius is governed by dual planets: Uranus and Saturn. Saturn then adds privation, obstacles, delay, hard work, pessimism, and research to the mix. This combination makes Aquarians society's seekers, political agitators, and revolutionaries. The Saturn influence of pessimism can also put a lot of challenges in front of them. The ruling planet of Uranus has a timid, abrupt, and sometimes aggressive nature, but also a visionary quality. They can perceive the future, and they know their life plan for years to come.
Symbol:	The glyph represents water and the flow of energy or wavelength. One of the few signs not represented by an animal, but instead by an element. The waves of water express the humanitarianism of this sign.

	Aquarius (cont.)
Personality & Outlook:	Connection is at the core of this sign but on the surface, they may not seem very emotional. However, this is usually because Aquarius is preoccupied with helping others and exchanging ideas. Highly intelligent, energetic, and talented, they often crave time alone just to sit and think. Without the ability to do they, they can become depressed. But in contrast, they dislike actually being lonely. This can also make them highly resentful if they believe their opinions are not valued. They can seem eccentric with their periods of intense self-reflection. You may see Aquarius running the gamut of emotional expressions from temperamental to uncompromising to aloof to lively. Deep thinkers, they are fascinated by gadgets and like to invent and tinker in the workshop. Without sufficient mental stimulation, they can become bored, and then they will lack motivation for a cause or project. Aquarius likes to fight for a cause, but can sometimes break promises to those involved. Although they have a reputation for being cold or distant, at least initially, they are actually generous with their time and resources. They just need to trust you before they express themselves. In searching for a cause, Aquarius can become too much of a dreamer, be unrealistic, or even impractical at times, losing touch with reality. Occasionally, even becoming fanatical in their views and destructive with their criticism.

Love/Relationship:	For those under this sign, intellectual stimulation is the best aphrodisiac. The best traits for a partner include good communication, imagination, openness, and a willingness to take risks. For a long-term relationship, integrity and honesty are the most essential traits. Once in love, they are totally committed, loyal, and will not be possessive.
Money/Job:	Career usually involves helping others as Aquarius are predominantly concerned with the welfare of others. They bring enthusiasm to whatever job they hold. Aquarius prefers a career that enables learning and development. Their intelligence, combined with a willingness to help out, inspires those around them. They are an unconventional type of visionary that likes to try to make humanity better. Careers that are a good fit: photography, pilot, teacher, writer, actor, but any situation where they can solve a problem without confines or guidelines may be enough to make any job desirable. Talented in balancing saving/spending money.

	Aquarius (cont.)
Family/Friends:	Very friendly and make friends everywhere they go. Great at networking. Friends and family of any Aquarius must have honesty and integrity, be creative and intelligent. Although they have a strong sense of duty to relatives, they will not maintain ties if those qualities are not met. Will do anything for a loved-one, including self-sacrifice. Aquarius corresponds to the Eleventh House (Friends House) which deals with social life, friendship, hopes, and wishes. Although Aquarius has a lot of friends, they also love to be by themselves, so a balance must be found. As they are very active and involved in social change, they will have a long list of people they know.
Possible Descriptors:	generous, patient, tolerant, friendly, unconventional, intelligent, energetic, talented, progressive, original, independent, aloof, philosophical, honest, humble, shy, driven, cautious, contrary, perverse, detached, eccentric, honest, forthright, reliable; tolerant, kind, considerate, helpful, withdrawn, , community-minded, humanitarian, impartial
Famous Aquarius:	Oprah Winfrey, Jennifer Aniston, Justin Timberlake, Alicia Keys, Bobby Brown, Sarah Palin, Michael Jordan, Ellen DeGeneres, Ed Sheeran, Shakira, John Travolta, Abraham Lincoln, Franklin Roosevelt, Ronald Reagan, Gertrude Stein, Charles Dickens, Christian Dior
Lucky Numbers:	4, 7, 11, 22, 29

PISCES-February 18 through March 20

Symbol:	Fish	**Quality**	Mutable
Day of the Week:	Thursday	**Ruling Planet:**	Neptune
Body Part:	Feet	**Secret Desire:**	To find unconditional love.
Gemstone:	Aquamarine or Bloodstone	**Color:**	mauve, lilac, purple, violet, sea green
Best Compatibility – Overall:	Virgo, Taurus	**Best Compatibility – Romantic:**	Taurus, Cancer, Scorpio, Capricorn
What they like:	laughing, romance, long letters, dancing, walking on the beach, being alone, music, spiritual themes, romance, visual media, swimming, and games of chance		
What they dislike:	barking orders, daylight, bad designs, reality, noisy music, criticism, replaying the past, cruelty, and people who are a "know-it-all"		
Element:	A Water Sign sometimes referred to as "The Flood," since they reach everyone without a convention and leaves their mark on others long after an encounter. As the third and final water sign, it blends the sentimentality of Cancer with Scorpio's force, creating an ocean of emotions. Emotional expression of creativity plays a big role.		

Quality:	Mutable signs: They know things must change and are comfortable with change. As a mutable Water Sign, Pisces explores and adjusts themselves to the feelings of those around them. This Sign will often offer advice, information or sympathy, whichever is most appropriate.
Ruling Planet:	Ruled by the planet Neptune: represents dreams, illusion, delusion, spirituality, theatrics, oneness, inspiration, deception, addictions. Neptune was the Greek god of the sea and renown for a furious temper. According to some, Pisces is ruled by dual planets, both Neptune and Jupiter. Jupiter deals with protection, expansiveness, generosity, opportunities, optimism, and luck.
Symbol:	Two fishes facing in opposite directions which show the duality of the Pisces nature. It can also show the plans lurking beneath the surface of this fantasy-oriented zodiac sign.
Personality & Outlook:	Pisces never like to see other people unhappy. Empathetic, they are driven to help those in need and can easily find themselves involved in someone else's drama. And by feeling things so deeply, this may lead them to become a constant worrier, which can then lead to indecision. Consequently, they may have a lack of follow-through because of an inability to make a decision. Can be serious daydreamers, but are generally very happy and vibrant. Pisces can be difficult to get to know, as they are frequently reticent to share things.
	Pisces (cont.)

Personality & Outlook (cont.):	Deeply religious, they can even sometimes be manic about their belief, which sometimes leads to bigotry or intolerance. Pisces generally don't like to hurt anyone's feelings and do not do well as leaders. Pisces are friendly, caring, intuitive, selfless, compassionate, and willing to help others. They may sometimes play the role of the victim or martyr in order to be the center of attention. Known to be one of the more tolerant signs, they are never judgmental and always forgiving. However, Pisces can be very secretive, deceptive, and calculating. As the final sign, some feel that this sign experiences the energy of all the other signs before it and are closest to the barrier between this world and the next. Can be very optimistic and love games of chance and can do well on stage dancing, singing, or acting; very big on participating or watching theater. Pisces can be easily discouraged and tend to give up easily in matters and can become very depressed due to their pessimistic outlook on life. Pisces can sometimes be easy to be persuaded, inspired, deceived, or convinced to buy something. Very impressionable, someone under this sign might give little or no resistance when they should. Consequently, they easily give in to temptation and lacks willpower.

Love/Relationship:	True romanticists, loyal, caring, gentle and unconditionally generous. Pisces are passionate lovers who want to feel a real connection. Short-term relationships are common. They can however, demonstrate jealousy on occasion. When it comes to love, Pisces' charisma plays a big part in their personality. Pisces has a sensitive nature and deep appreciation for the inner qualities of their lover. Those under this sign are the happiest when they are in a loving relationship or involved in a creative project. Pisces enjoys the romance, courting, dating, and everything in-between when beginning a relationship.

	Pisces (cont.)
Money/Job:	Dedicated, Pisces will stay with one company for decades even if they are not completely happy there. They do the best in a career that allows them to use creative skill and to work with a charity. Good career choices include attorney, musician, social worker, veterinarian, salesperson, architect, or game designer. May work with charities or lost causes since they feel the need to make changes to the lives of others. Any non-profit would be lucky to have them as they are great problem-solvers, hard-working, dedicated, and reliable. They don't think much about money or making it, but see it as a means to achieving their goals. With spending habits, they can go down either path, either spending too much carelessly or spending nothing and being miserable.

Family/Friends:	Pisces can be the best friends you'll ever have, and they will put the needs of their friends and family members above their own needs. Loyal, devoted, compassionate, gentle and caring, your Pisces friend will try to resolve any problems as best they can. And don't think that you can hide it from them because they will intuitively sense if something is wrong. They are very expressive and will share their feelings with everyone around them, and they expect everyone they know to be as open as they are. Frequent and easy communication with friends and family is essential. Since they have an intuitive understanding of the life cycle, they achieve the best emotional relationships.
Possible Descriptors:	dreamy, deceptive, considerate, loving, affectionate, imaginative, intuitive, trustworthy, psychic, supportive, creative, artistic, broad-minded, tolerant, talented, secretive, calculating, creative, loyal, daydreamer, happy, vibrant, sympathetic, emotional, kind, earnest, idealistic, faithful , opportunistic, indolent, withdrawn
Famous Pisces:	Albert Einstein, Rihanna, Justin Bieber, Adam Levin, Carrie Underwood, Kesha, Steve Jobs, Kurt Cobain, Eva Longoria, Drew Barrymore, George Washington, Andrew Jackson, Victor Hugo, Dr. Seuss, Henrik Ibsen
Lucky Numbers:	3, 9, 12, 15, 18, 24

Chapter 2 Relationship Astrology:

Signs with the same element can understand each other the best. However, there are complementary elements as well: Air blends well with Fire, Water with Earth. The strongest attraction usually lies with the opposing sign.

Aries: Aquarius, Gemini, Leo, and Sagittarius

Aquarius: The combination of the vision of an Aquarius and the action of an Aries makes a very creative match. The relationship will not be dull as each can be quite competitive. They communicate really well. Both crave excitement and new experiences but understand the other's idealistic and enthusiastic outlook on life. The admiration between the two is mutual; Aries loves how unique Aquarius is, and Aquarius enjoys Aries energy. The connection is undeniable, but so are the differences as well. An Aries can think that their Aquarius partner can be too unpredictable and Aries can be too possessive. Both partners must keep reassuring the other that everything is secure and the relationship is important.

Gemini: They have a connection on a physical and intellectual level. They are a lot alike in which both are active and optimistic. These signs typically have great communication and thoroughly understand each other. Gemini values independence and will admire Aries's independent spirit. Arguments may arise if Aries becomes too controlling or takes Gemini's flirtatious nature too seriously. Together, they are well balanced. Aries wants to do new things and Gemini wants to talk about them. Both signs have lots of energy, and Gemini's intelligence and ability to see all sides of a task will help Aries who loves to get started on projects full steam ahead. While Gemini may waver on what projects to start, Aries is able to make the decision and can keep things on task. Although both are ruled by planets representing communication, they approach it differently.

Leo: Sparks fly between an Aries and a Leo. Fire Signs, both of them, are passionate, energetic, and competitive which means that there is a lot of action in this match. Since both Signs want to be in charge, this can create problems, but they have respect and admiration for each other. If they can simply take turns being in charge, they will have a more harmonious relationship. With fiery passion and a competition for domination, this match can be full of drama. Both proud and impatient, further drama can surface as Leo likes to have their egos stroked, but as this may bore Aries, they may not oblige. Leos are a flirt and may cause more drama. Despite these differences, Leo can be a great counselor for Aries. Both Aries and Leo are ruled by masculine energy planets archetypes, so they understand each other, since they come from the same place.

<u>Sagittarius</u>: These partners have much in common and are very compatible, both being pioneers and explorers. They both crave adventure and new experiences, but this could be a match prone to accidents. Sagittarius may overlook little details, and Aries is always in a rush. But boredom may set in as both signs have energy to start new things, but then may become bored and never finish anything. Aries and Sagittarius can make both great friends and terrific lovers. Since both are optimistic, problems are rare, but the need for independence can cause strife. Sagittarius has an even greater need for independence than Aries does. Although both signs are quick to forgive, Aries can be a bit more sensitive. Sagittarius occasionally speaks without thinking first and can spend some time apologizing for that.

Taurus: Pisces and Virgo

<u>Pisces</u>: This is generally a happy union. Taurus is practical while Pisces is idealistic. Both signs are nurturers and both value stability and harmony. Pisces dreams and Taurus provides the grounding. Pisces offers kindness and gentleness which Taurus appreciates in a lover. When Venus (Taurus) and Neptune (Pisces) meet, a lovely spiritual bond is made. Both with feminine energy, together they epitomize an idealistic relationship, bordering on heavenly. However, this kind of dreamy combination can end up being a thing of illusion and fantasy.

Virgo: A match between a Taurus and a Virgo is a practical match. Both Signs value practicality in every aspect of their daily lives. Sincere and devoted to each other, both have a lot of integrity. Taurus likes Virgo's quick mind while Virgo appreciates Taurus's strength. This relationship can take a while to develop since Virgo is cautious, but with the foundation, both are in it long-term. These two Signs value common sense and the practicality along with being materialistic. Virgo's tendency to analyze can lead to criticism and Taurus may take it too seriously. And Virgo may be annoyed by Taurus's stubborn nature, which may cause Virgo to criticize more frequently. Neither should take the other too seriously.

Gemini: Aquarius and Libra and sometimes other Gemini

Aquarius: This pair can create quite a stimulating mental connection; Aquarius is full of ideas and Geminis love that. Both will need their independence; but since it is mutual, they will both understand this requirement. Aquarius may sometimes feel that Gemini drags their feet a little too much and Gemini may feel that Aquarius is a little too stubborn. But neither of these should manifest as major problems. In general, they understand each other and mesh well.

Both have a great deal of energy and their minds are quick, sharing new and better ideas. With Aquarius' willpower, they will be more likely to put their ideas into action. Both Signs just hate wasting time, and Aquarius will help Gemini to focus but must be careful to give Gemini plenty of space and freedom, as a Gemini doesn't like to feel pushed into anything.

Gemini: Two Geminis are really like four people forming a bond, and will never be boring. Both will have the same need for intellectual stimulation, and will almost always be talking, but it will work by a constant exchange of ideas. Two Geminis together will be all about freedom and communication and may end up being the most favorite couple in their circle of friends. Avoiding competition and cooperating will ensure the relationship goes more smoothly and both remain happy.

Libra: A personality of two halves loves the balance that Libra has. And Libra will be interested in the talkative, smart aspects of Gemini. While Gemini focuses on ideas, Libra loves beauty and art. So, a trip to an art museum and then coffee afterward to discuss would be their perfect afternoon. Both have a lot of mental energy and can brainstorm all sorts of great ideas when they come together. Luckily, Libra also has the initiative to put ideas into action, which is something the Gemini may be lacking in.

Cancer: Pisces and Scorpio

Pisces: Both Cancer and Pisces are sympathetic and tolerant. Pisces can get energized by Cancer's ideas. Cancer can guide fanciful Pisces with their practical nature and Pisces can show Cancer a world of spirituality and creativity. While Pisces will have a minimal amount of stuff, Cancer loves possessions, desiring comfort and luxury. Although this may seem as they would be at odds, the emotional depth shared by Cancer and Pisces can make it a highly rewarding match.

Scorpio: Both intense energy Signs, they can combine well with each partner's strengths balancing the weaknesses of the other. A relationship between these two will usually be heightened by a strong sexual attraction. Cancer and Scorpio usually have a great deal in common, which provides the potential to keep a relationship passionate and strong. Cancer and Scorpio like a comfortable home and will enjoy buying things together to create that space. Scorpio strives for power while Cancer likes security. Since they are both focused on their family and their home, they complement each other well.

Leo: Aries, Gemini, Libra and Sagittarius

Aries: Both are Fire Signs, that are competitive, so they both want to be in charge. This may either create a lot of passion or a lot of conflict. Both can be proud, impatient and dominant. Since Leo is a flirt and needs to be adored, Aries may get annoyed or bored with this.

Gemini: This union will be playful, hopeful, and high-spirited. Since Leo is dramatic and creative, Gemini will be satisfied with the mental stimulation from the pair. But, even though Leo is also a flirt, they may not like Gemini's desire to also do so. And if Gemini believes that Leo is trying to exhibit too much control over the relationship, conflict may erupt. Their differences in approaching a problem – intellectual versus instinctual – may cause some arguments as well.

Libra: An agreeable love match. Since they are two signs apart, they will have a deep understanding. Libra's harmony will counterbalance Leo's energy. Libra's charm and tact can also help to temper Leo's more direct and acerbic personality.

Sagittarius: Dynamic and full of life, this couple is fun to be around. Each encourages the other to reach for the stars. Both extremely social, they will want to be the leaders in their group of friends.

Virgo: Capricorn and Taurus

Capricorn: Virgo will love Capricorn's intensity while Capricorn will adore Virgo's attention to detail and intuition. A smart and very rational pairing. Their foundation will lay both of their realistic approach and a need for material security. Neither will let their emotions get the better of them and will exhibit admirable dedication to achieving goals.

Taurus: Practical is the key word here. Since Virgo is cautious by nature, any relationship between the two may take some time to develop. Both enjoy the finer things in life, but will work hard to earn them. Virgo's quick mind will complement Taurus' strength and dedication.

But Virgo's thoughts may lead to criticism and this may weigh too heavily on Taurus. And Taurus' stubborn nature may be a stumbling block for Virgo. Each must learn to not be quite so serious.

Libra: Leo and Sagittarius

<u>Leo</u>: Two signs apart in the Zodiac makes them a delightful pair. Libra's harmony will balance Leo's energy. Each will appreciate the contrasting aspects of the other and benefit from them. For example, Leo's more caustic and direct personality will be smoothed by Libra's good manners and charm. Leo will help Libra make decisions while Libra will help more whims.

<u>Sagittarius</u>: With signs that are two signs apart in the Zodiac, this is a harmonious romance. Libra appreciates art and beauty; Sagittarius is always searching for more experiences and knowledge. Exploring an art museum in a new town is a terrific first date. The relationship will stay in its romantic stage longer as this pair will keep things fresh and exciting. Libra may get their feelings hurt occasionally when Sagittarius speaks without thinking. And Sagittarius may feel a little boxed in emotionally. But Libra's diplomacy will smooth things over quickly.

Scorpio: Pisces and Scorpio

<u>Pisces</u>: Both water elements, they have a lot of respect for each other. Pisces is gentle and kind which Scorpio will greatly admire. Idealistic, Pisces can sometimes withdraw into their own selves, a trait which Scorpio will understand. Scorpio may help Pisces to turn some of their dreams into reality. Minor conflict may occur if Scorpio gets too dedicated to material

possessions and doesn't give Pisces the freedom to devote to charity. Long-term ambitions are almost completely dissimilar, but knowing this, they can work together to form a plan for the both of them.

Scorpio: A perfect passionate storm. May become obsessed with one another and the relationship will advance quickly. It will be an all-or-nothing proposition – the best relationship ever, or the most destructive. The intensity of the love match makes their shared power unconquerable as long as their combined energy and passion aren't self-destructing.

Sagittarius: Aquarius, Aries, Leo and Libra

Aquarius: This will be a unique and creative union. A close friendship will exist underneath this good love pairing, even if their spirit of competition will need close monitoring. With the signs two signs apart on the Zodiac, there is an excellent rapport. These two will enjoy good times together since they are both idealistic and excited about life. With both signs valuing their independence, they will work together to ensure they are a team. Communication would be a key to happiness.

Aries: These two have a lot in common and are very compatible. Always ready for a new adventure, they desire lots of life experiences. But, since they rush into things and overlook details, they may suffer some accidents. Their biggest challenge may be making the relationship into a long-term arrangement. Both will forgive and forget quickly, so they won't hold long-term grudges.

Leo: These signs are very dynamic and live life fully. Each one with encourage their partner to soar. People will enjoy being with these couple as they both are charming and charismatic. Leo will want to be in control while Sagittarius will want to examine the nuances and plan an approach.

<u>Libra</u>: Two signs apart on the Zodiac, this pair exists in agreement. Sagittarius is always in search of learning and Libra has an appreciation for pretty things. Since Sagittarius likes to travel and explore, Libra will be a good companion for new sights. Their relationship will remain in the romance stage longer as they are both optimistic and will work to keep things exciting. Libra is a diplomat and will work to resolve any conflict and both are rather quick to forgive any slight rather quickly.

Capricorn: Pisces, Scorpio, Taurus, and Virgo

Pisces: This may seem to be a case of "opposites attract," and this relationship may develop slowly and will get stronger over time. They will be honest with each other devoted to the relationship. Capricorn will appreciate Pisces' sweet nature; Pisces will be attracted to Capricorn's wittiness and stubbornness. Difficulties may occur if Capricorn dominates Pisces's sensitive side, but Pisces should understand that this is just Capricorn's style, but not a personal attack. The best part is their unique blend of temperaments.

Scorpio: As neither sign is quick to open their hearts, this relationship may take awhile to get off the ground. But, once they are comfortable with each other and trust, they will find they have an intense connection of loyalty and of friendship. Capricorn, capable and stable, will help to calm Scorpio's hot-headed temperament. But they must not be too stable or placid as Scorpio enjoys intense emotional connection. And those emotions may teach Capricorn to look below the surface of life. As goal-oriented signs, if they make their relationship a goal, there will be success.

Taurus: Realistic, dependable and conservative, these two signs seem to be two peas in a pod. However, at their core, they can seem quite different. Capricorn can see Taurus as too lazy since they are not as focused on career and success. Taurus can find Capricorn a little too restrained and traditional. But, if they can meet in the middle and each learn a little something from the other, the relationship will benefit. Their similar values may be enough to bridge any gap.

Virgo: A strong foundation of a union of brains. These signs are smart, realistic, and rational. They expect a lot of themselves and out of others. Capricorn will respect Virgo's intuition while Virgo will appreciate Capricorn's intensity. Both enjoy material security and won't let their emotions get the better of them. Dedicated to each other with similar goas, their mutual interests can make this a relationship with a future.

Aquarius: Gemini and Libra

<u>Gemini</u>: Seems like a perfect match: Geminis love ideas and Aquarius is usually full of wonderfully visionary ideas. Both with a strong need for independence and lots of energy, they will recognize and respect that quality in their partner. Conflict may arise if Gemini seems too flighty for fast-moving Aquarius; or if Aquarius seems to stubborn for Gemini. They are great at working together and will be a veritable think-tank for great ideas.

<u>Libra</u>: These two signs seem to connect on a higher mental plane, sharing a love of culture, people, and art/beauty. With a similar level of commitment to a relationship, they will not be unbalanced by one partner being needier than the other. Energetic and enthusiastic, they will enjoy being together and doing new things, especially if that activity can bring a positive change to the world. Aquarius, the most progressive mind of the Zodiac, when combined with diplomatic Libra, can be a great addition to any worthy cause.

Pisces: Cancer and Scorpio

<u>Cancer</u>: A balance of the practical and the spiritual. Cancer can help dreamy Pisces bring their dreams to life; Pisces can offset Cancer's practicality with a little daydreaming. Conflict may occur if Cancer, who loves material possessions, doesn't understand or respect the Spartan lifestyle that their Pisces partner prefers. Their shared emotional connection may overcome any differences in goals and lifestyles. They will rotate on the

role of teacher or student as both have a great capacity for compassion and emotions and will teach their partners and the world.

<u>Scorpio</u>: Two water elements, these signs are intuitive and in touch with human nature. This partnership will be a blending of mind and heart. With Scorpio's tendency to be secretive, Pisces may be a good sign to pair with this, as they will understand having their own need to withdraw into their own minds occasionally. Scorpio may help Pisces to turn some dreams into reality and provide the foundation for the relationship to be built on. Pisces, more in tune with emotions and spirituality can show Scorpio a world of sympathy and kindness. If they can overcome what may seem like different long-term plans, this can be a very rewarding romance with a profound connection and commitment.

Chapter 3: Finding Yourself through Your Zodiac and Growing on a Spiritual Level

Astrology is considered by most people to be a superstitious guide to everyday life. But, in reality, it can be a very deep subject. If used only for guidance in mundane matters, you will not be utilizing astrology for all of its teachings. Philosophically and mathematically speaking, astrology is a vast network of information that can provide profound understanding. Historically, astrology was used primarily as a guide to spiritual development and was considered a divine science. Although a science, once an astrologer begins to make predictions and classifications of human behavior, it crosses into a psychological or metaphysical field. If those predictions are reliable and unchanging, then this further emphasizes the metaphysical aspects of the practice. Scientifically, there is not proven, causal relationship between any one given planet and the way someone falls in love. However, it can be a technique for interpreting a situation in relation to the universe as a whole. Astrology can provide the clues to discovering the meaning of any situation and the way the factors of any situation operate. This can be the reason that people who struggle with traditional spiritual and rules can turn to astrology. Everyone is seeking answers to "why" and "how," and the signs may provide guidance without restriction.

According to a New York Post article, more than half of the millennial generation believes in astrology as a science. This is compared to only eight (8) percent of the Chines public. This can include other metaphysical services such as tarot card, aura reading, astrology, mediums, and palmistry. One theory is that the lack of structure in the field of astrology may be exactly what is desirable about it for them.

However, with astrology, man can study the influence of the planets and further investigate the link between all aspects of creation. Astrology is meant to assist man with their inner journey, allowing people to become more aware of how the universe can impact all aspects of existence. The relation of the planets and stars to the human existence, mind, and body is very subtle.

A person is born on a specific time and day and is established into an astrological sign, house, cusp or other designation. To fully reflect on the traits and predilections of those under that category, you can investigate and strive to completely understand your relationship with the universe. This can be especially useful by raising your awareness of the past and the potential of the future and can finesse your inner attunement with God. However, approaching astrology as a superstition can limit the use of this information and change this resource to a passive dependence on fate while you wait for the planets or stars to shift positions. Some people believe that religion and astrology cannot exist together as God is the only one who can have power or influence over your lifestyle, personality, and future. Under this argument, if you are spiritual and can actually commune with God to receive answers on how you should behave and what your path is in life, there is no need for anything like astrology to guide you. Others believe that astrology can simply give you more information about your journey in this world and also with God, giving you further understanding and knowledge of yourself and those you interact with every day. Or it may separate from spirituality completely and use astrology as a way to dissect and study the universe as it exists only through a cycle of cosmic principles and energy. Any one of these approaches is a personal interpretation that everyone must make on their own.

However, it can be argued that the use of astrology as a superstition can make someone into an automaton who is slavishly dependent on readings of the stars and positions of the planets. Those that argue this position indicate that allegiance to the Creator of the universe is the one true way and should be lead by the spirit and not by the material world. By delving deeply into your own divine nature, you may uncover deeper levels within yourself that will enable you to rise above all karmic realities.

Those in support of using astrology believe that the zodiac signs were developed by God to reveal information and teach us. Since God created the stars and planets and the zodiac signs are based on those, there is a synergy that exists. Awareness and correction of our weaknesses and strength can give us a greater sense of our behavior and tune us into improving.

Taoism of Chinese culture is very closely associated with the zodiac. This religion believes that things in space can change a person's destiny and constellations and space can be used to show that future. The sun was an integral part of the calculations of the zodiac as well. Many signs are discussed as being a "yin" or "yang" sign, and this originates with Taoism. This represents any two opposing principles of the universe and is the basis for how everything works. When combined, the yin-yang can change the characteristics of the twelve zodiac animals.

Another example of a religion that ties to the zodiac is Buddhism. Legend tells how Buddha chose all of the animals for the zodiac. This religion is popular in Chinese culture and has had a big effect on how the zodiac was structured and the role it now plays in modern-day religion. But there are some historical and astrological evidence that the religions of Christianity, Judaism, Paganism, Hinduism, Taoism, Zoroastrianism, Jainism, Islam, and Buddhism all share some similarities with each other and astrological science.

- Christianity: The central belief of Christianity is that Jesus Christ is the Son of God and the Savior (Messiah). Christians have faith that Jesus was anointed as the savior of humanity by God and believe that Jesus' life and crucifixion were the fulfillment of prophecies contained in the Old Testament.

- Judaism: This is characterized by the belief of one transcendent God who revealed himself to Moses, Abraham, and the Hebrew prophets and by a religious life in accordance with rabbinic traditions and scripture.

- Paganism: This is a polytheistic religion that focuses on sensual pleasures and material goods. This is a movement to revive nature-worshiping, pre-Christian religion and other nature-based spiritual paths. This definition may be a larger umbrella term for similar groups such as Wicca and Neo-Druidism.

- Hinduism: The major beliefs and principles of Hinduism include the four aims of human life (Purusartha) specifically: Artha (work, prosperity, and wealth), Dharma (duties/ethics), Kama (passions/desires), and Moksha (freedom and liberation) along with Karma, Samsara, and Yogas.
- Taoism: A Chinese philosophy denoting the fundamental or true nature of the world with a selflessness and simplicity in

conformity with the Tao. A life expressing the essence of spontaneity and leading a life of non-purposive action. Taoism arose around the same time as Confucianism.

- Zoroastrianism: Zoroaster taught the existence of demons, angels, and saviors, similar ideas which can also be found in Judaism, Christianity, and Islam. The Avesta is their sacred text and contains rituals, hymns, and spells against demons.

- Jainism: This is a non-theistic religion founded in the 6th century BC in India as a reaction against the orthodox teachings of Brahmanism, and still practiced there. The Jain religion teaches reincarnation and salvation by perfection through those successive lives, and doing no harm to living creatures, and is noted for its ascetics.

- Islam: Someone who follows or practices Islam is called a Muslim which is a monotheistic, Abrahamic religion. Muslims read the Quran as their holy book and consider it to be the verbatim word of Allah as revealed to the Islamic messenger and prophet, Muhammad.
-
- Buddhism: This is a religion where truth is paramount. A practitioner is always striving to achieve the state of truth and is aware of the suffering of this world. People who worship Buddhism don't believe that their actual god is Buddha. To them, Buddha is a representation as a human who achieves the enlightenment phase and sees how the mind truly works. They believe that a person changers when they have this knowledge. Achieving total enlightenment is called "nirvana."

Under the teachings of astrology, each of the signs has a way they prefer living their lives and a type of belief system that speaks to them. In general, Air and Water signs are more spiritual, and Fire and Earth signs are more committed to a structured or specific religion. Each sign has different needs and abilities and may be more inclined to follow a spiritual belief system that connects to their basic outlook.

Aries: A Fire Sign ruled by the planet Mars may need a physical spiritual practice, but with control. Yoga may be suited to this temperament, especially those types that are more energetic or vigorous in practice.

Taurus: An Earth Sign ruled by artistic Venus that brings out a gentle and creative approach to life. Most Taurus enjoy being in nature. This may lead them to feel a close connection to the Pagan religion. The celebrations throughout the year combining the spiritual with feasts and celebrations will speak directly to the heart of a Taurus. Having a close connection to the planet makes anyone under this Earth sign more enthusiastic.

Gemini: The planet Mercury rules this Air Sign. Gemini needs to be constantly busy mentally. This allows them to be more open to alternative approaches and spiritual discipline. The practice of mindful meditation, a Buddhist tradition, may help to quiet the mind and bring peace. With too much taxing the mind, the body can suffer as the nervous system can be pushed into insomnia and anxiety. The practice of turning off the brain and focusing on deeper connections is a great way to deal with stress.

Cancer: A Water Sign influence by the Moon, Cancer individuals can display a higher level of psychic awareness than other signs, especially if they have a history or family ancestors with similar abilities. Psychic pursuits, clairvoyance, aura readings, and other similar fields may tune into the abilities and penchant of Cancer.

Leo: A Fire Sign ruled by the Sun, Leos have a lot of energy and need to be active daily. A spiritual practice that may appeal to them and which suits their temperament would be Tai Chi. Tai Chi is strongly linked to the Chinese philosophy and martial arts. It adds strength to the posture, deepens the breathing, and has many health benefits. Leos will enjoy Tai Chi classes more over practicing alone as those will ad a social aspect to it as well.

Virgo: An Earth Sign ruled by Mercury, Virgos need to be careful to engage in regular exercise and follow a diet. As their nervous system is an area of concern, they will benefit from regular practice. Alternative sources such as spiritual healing, aura reading, or Reiki can be beneficial to this sign. Essentially, when participating in a spiritual activity, Virgos need activities that do not overly use their minds but can bring themselves out. It is assumed that among the twelve signs, Virgo is the natural healer. Virgo likes to give advice and service, so any spiritual or religious practice that includes doing good works would be close to their heart. However, any spiritual practice for a Virgo should allow them to recharge their mental batteries.

Libra: An Air Sign ruled by Venus, balance is their trademark. The study of auras might interest a Libra. Auras are the field that surrounds the physical body and are typically different colors which can display physical health, emotional well-being, and spirituality. The study and recognition of auras may allow a Libra to better understand the actions of others and teach them how to become more balanced when dealing with the other people in their lives. In turn, this may help them to build better relationships with people around them.

Scorpio: A Water Sign ruled by Pluto, a spiritual journey will come as second nature to a Scorpio. During their lifetime, they may investigate a number of religions until they identify closely with one. With a drive to understand their life path and human psychology, they may experiment divination practice with Tarot to address the choices people face every day and properly decide on options that will make them move forward. The mysterious nature of the Tarot may appeal to a Scorpio to delve into the hidden aspects of the universe and life and to further understand the reason of why people live and thrive on Earth.

Sagittarius: A Fire Sign ruled by Jupiter, this sign is known as the philosopher of the zodiac. They may be drawn to philosophy or a teaching role in whatever religion they choose. As they enjoy studying and exploring new ways of thinking and then sharing those words of wisdom, they may indeed venture into being a spiritual leader. Their journey into spirituality may involve Christianity, Hindu, Buddhism, or other alternative religion.

Capricorn: An Earth Sign ruled by Saturn, although a materialistic sign, Capricorn does have the spiritual virtues that are required for a spiritual journey. Individuals in this sign need a spirituality that is going to last, combining both the need for being alone and spiritual advancement. Although less widely known, one option may be Shamanism. A Shaman alters the state of consciousness to communicate with the power of animals and the spirit world. Shamanism originates in central and northern Asia. This ancient and powerful spiritual practice takes time to learn, which will ensure a connection with Capricorn.

Aquarius: An Air Sign ruled by Uranus, Aquarius is always looking up at the stars and to the future. Those under this sign may indeed be inclined to astrology. For those under this sign, astrology may be the key to self-understanding. Following astrology and finding the pattern through the planets and constellations may be a source of guidance to an Aquarius. Once this pattern is revealed, an Aquarian delves into a journey of joy and fulfillment and can take that lost knowledge to others.

Pisces: A Water Sign ruled by Neptune, a Pisces personality constitutes their journey through their life and their spirituality. As the last sign of the zodiac, the Pisces understands it is only a small distance away to the next world. Pisces can contact the dead and possesses incredible physic awareness. The Pisces need to learn self discipline by energy cleaning and meditation. They are very sensitive with the surroundings and those that they come in with. To help steady their energy, it is best to give them some time to recuperate and be creative. This can lead them to a number of spiritual pursuits that connect them to that awareness such as reiki healing, aura cleansing, meditation, and more.

Chapter 4: How You Can Strengthen Your Relationships and Friendships by Reading the Zodiac Signs

When you explore astrology and see what traits and tendencies are common to each of the zodiac signs. You can then be prepared when dealing with friends, coworkers, managers, lovers and potential mates. Knowing the traits of others can help us to be better prepared to accept the flaws and all. And that's really what most people would like to experience – being accepted. As such, we can use the following information to prepare for interactions with a certain zodiac sign in our lives.

An ARIES BOSS: They are born leaders, but can be demanding. They provide clear instructions that are explicit. Aries can enjoy making decisions and seeing their plans implemented. They like individuality for themselves and others.

An ARIES EMPLOYEE: They are good at following rules and taking direction from supervisors. But they will quickly recognize any shortcomings of their supervisors. They will be quiet and hard-working until some small item sets them off. Aries employees will be full of suggestions to improve how things are done.

An ARIES ROMANCE: Noted for their honesty. They love close involvement with their romantic partner. But they also need a partner with lots of energy to keep up with them. Aries partners can be independent but will want daily contact. Make sure to never call them needy, but they feel the need to be very connected to their partners. Make sure to listen to their needs, feelings, and advice.

An ARIES SPOUSE: Honesty is prized; an Aries will expect to be forgiven if they stray. Since they are career-oriented, they may lean more towards their career than family. A spouse will need to ensure things run smoothly at home. However, they are not exceptional housekeepers/cleaners.

An ARIES FRIEND: Friends are faithful but may only contact their friends as frequently as every few months. Your Aries friend will be busy and may not have a lot of time to interact. If you are an Aries' oldest friend, you may even get included in family celebrations making you that important.

An ARIES PARENT: Sometimes too involved in their children's lives, Aries parents have strong ethical beliefs and will not be very tolerant of breaking rules. They must remember to allow their kids to try, fail and learn.

An ARIES CHILD: Childhood is a very big part to Aries, as long as the parents don't over-burden their children with adult responsibilities. An Aries child is best left alone with the security to express themselves without being condemned.

A TAURUS BOSS: The Taurus boss can be bossy, but will stay behind the scenes as long as their employees are well trained. They will take the time to explain their expectations. All rules will be minimal, but the rules are also considered to be concrete.

A TAURUS EMPLOYEE: Very work-oriented, but sometimes more oriented on personal comfort, making their progress on a task is slower. They are good at procrastination and will respond better to a gentle reminder than sharp orders.

A TAURUS ROMANCE: A Taurus tends to be possessive and may treat a partner as something that belongs to them. However, they will see this as a positive reflection of how much they love you. Conflict may arise if you try to be independent and not agree with everything your Taurus asks.

A TAURUS SPOUSE: Taurus spouse is caring, devoted, dependable, stable, and usually the dominant partner. They enjoy being the head of the household. They like to make most of the big decisions. Taurus spouses can procrastinate but once they decide, there is not stopping them. They love pleasure: food, sex, and other sensual pleasures.

A TAURUS FRIEND: They are always faithful and will help as much as possible. But they may not be the best source of useful advice. They see things in black and white, so their vision may not be skewed. Fun to be with, Taurus friends enjoy entertainment. But you must be careful not to take advantage of their generous nature.

A TAURUS PARENT: They love being parents as they are nurturers. Taurus parents enjoy large families. They struggle to love unconditionally, so they may not be able to support their children unless certain conditions are met. Consequently, their children may not trust promises or generosity.

A TAURUS CHILD: A child of this Sign can be of a serious nature. Since they interpret things literally, they will expect parents and authority figures to keep their promises. They will be a complex combination of talking and silence; active and lazy; excited and aloof – which makes their moods hard to read moods. They will be unhappy if they do not have their own stuff. A Taurus child will share their toys, but only on their terms.

A GEMINI BOSS: A Gemini boss is comfortable with giving orders and coordinating. They like being part of a team as it allows them to share experiences. They are not born leaders, preferring to be a "hands off" leader. Gemini is very good at delegating but likes to have the final say.

A GEMINI EMPLOYEE: They love to be busy, and they are very good at multi-tasking. They love to think up new approaches to old projects. But Geminis get bored easily and may lack follow-through on long-term projects. They are usually particularly adroit manually.

A GEMINI ROMANCE: Will definitely add excitement to your life, but also some uncertainty. It may be difficult to predict their moods. Gemini may sometimes flake on appointments. They will be fascinating but may also be aggravating.

A GEMINI SPOUSE: They will need individuality and freedom. They may create problems with stability in the marriage. A Gemini spouse may get double standards in place when they feel they deserve more freedom than their spouses. Usually, don't think what they are doing is ever wrong morally. Must have a strong spouse that stands up to them.

A GEMINI FRIEND: They are more fun to be around when things are going well. They are susceptible to stress out when it comes to emergencies. If you want to have a good time, invite along a Gemini. They will provide lots of chatter, so be prepared to listen.

A GEMINI PARENT: They will offer their children a wide variety of interests and stimulation. They are good parents when they are interested and engaged. They enjoy their role as the family leader. But they may be too preoccupied with the stuff in their own minds to be a caretaker whole-heartedly all the time, so kids must be prepared to take care of themselves. Geminis are susceptible to worry and stress.

A GEMINI CHILD: Needs lots of parental input. They will display a lot of interest over a lot of different subjects. They should have a great deal of stimulation to keep them engaged. They will range from an easy child to a very challenging one based on possible stimulation and moods.

A CANCER BOSS: They are very particular about how things get done. They can be demanding. They want things to run smoothly and they like their dominance to be unquestioned. Rules are not as important as the team but do not underestimate the dominant qualities of a Cancer boss.

A CANCER EMPLOYEE: They are best at a desk job if they are not interrupted, they can produce a lot of paperwork. A Cancer employee possesses a good loyalty to the company they work for. They will play things close to the vest, watching, listening, and learning. Thus, their opinions are worth listening to.

A CANCER ROMANCE: They like steady, reliable relationship. Since they like habits, they like their partners to be available to them on a regular basis. They will count on them for everything. A Cancer partner can be cuddly as long as they are getting their way. If not, they may come across as crabby or withdrawn. They are very self-protective.

A CANCER SPOUSE: They like to have security at home. Since a Cancer spouse will spend a lot of time at home, they like their house "just so." They may spend too much money on home furnishings or improvements.

A CANCER FRIEND: They will work to keep their friends to themselves and not share. They want to know you are their best friend. They are good listeners, but will probably not share a lot of their own personal information.

A CANCER PARENT: Loving and caring parents that are both affectionate and protective. But, a Cancer parent can sometimes become over-protective, it can be a hard lesson for them to learn on how to let go a little.

A CANCER CHILD: Can become overly dependent on their parents. They need security and a great deal of support and guidance from their parents. Developing their own independence is a Cancer child's challenge.

A LEO BOSS: Is a born leader. The Leo enjoys being the head of the company. Leo bosses are fair as long as their authority is not being challenged. They believe they are simply trying to stand up for the working conditions of their employees. They take great pride in their work.

A LEO EMPLOYEE: Will be faithful to the company to the point of becoming a workaholic. They will stick faithfully to a job or a task. However, they will be resistant to change. Ambition will often push a Leo up the corporate ladder.

A LEO ROMANCE: Your girlfriend/boyfriend will be committed, supportive, and enthusiastic. But try not to impinge on their ambitious career plans; never make them choose between their relationship and career path. Although they hate to see a relationship end, they will have the confidence to move on with someone new.

A LEO SPOUSE: They are loyal, but may not remain faithful if their spouse seems distant. In order to be happy in marriage, Leo needs to be treated like royalty and put up on a pedestal. Since Leos are good at acting, they can pretend to be happily married for years just for the sake of the children involved, family or status.

A LEO FRIEND: They are excellent at making friends. Their loyalty and devotion are marks of their good friendship. They are not overly needy, so they can do without contact on a regular basis. However, when contacted, they prefer an in-person, close-up check-in rather than a phone call or text.

A LEO PARENT: Fiercely protective of their children, but they may go overboard as they think they always know better. Since their careers are important, they may not always be present as a parent. Leo parents may lean heavily on daycare, preschools, grandparents, and other assistants in child care.

A LEO CHILD: Will feel that caregivers are lucky to have them in their lives. They are confident and strong and self-assured. They will be accomplished in what activities they participate in. May not be inclined to academia, but will contribute to politics, activities, and sports.

A VIRGO BOSS: Realistic and practical, so results will be important to this boss. Data supporting any position or argument will greatly improve your chances of convincing them in an argument. Emotions do not play well, so stick with logic. A Virgo boss will not appreciate wasting time.

A VIRGO EMPLOYEE: They will take their work seriously. Dependable and trustworthy, they can sometimes be a little dull. Since they are private people, work can be a good social outlet, so much so that they frequently find that a co-worker ends up being their best friend.

A VIRGO ROMANCE: They are very good at planning. Their talents are best utilized by putting them in charge of setting up the yearly vacation or complicated outings. But, they may put more focus into the relationship rather than the person they are actually with.

A VIRGO SPOUSE: Good at marriage and homemaking but can get too insistent on order. This may drive their spouse crazy. In contrast to their need for order, their personal space may be rather sloppy (to you, but there is an order in the mess for them). They shine when it comes to emergency situations.

A VIRGO FRIEND: Supportive and helpful, they seem to intuitively know when you need them. They may seem needy, but they have trouble asking for help. Constant contact is not necessary, but make sure you check in periodically.

A VIRGO PARENT: They like making rules and are big on structure. This may create conflict as the child seeks independence, especially during the power struggle of adolescence.

A VIRGO CHILD: They are dutiful but resentful and may grow out of control if they feel unappreciated. The reward for helpfulness should be considered as they respond to this. They have highly judgmental and critical side. There will be long-term issues if the parent doesn't keep promises made to the Virgo child.

A LIBRA BOSS: They need to believe they are well-liked by their employees. Sometimes, they make them focus more on popularity than performance. Those who know that may manipulate that weakness.

A LIBRA EMPLOYEE: They prefer to work alone since they may have problems concentrating when surrounded by distractions. They can be perfectionists. Colleagues may value them for their understanding nature.

A LIBRA ROMANCE: They are choosy about who is on their arm: what they look like, sound like, and behave like. They expect to be treated well, but may not consider reciprocating. Problems arise when Libras are unhappy, so issues should be addressed immediately.

A LIBRA SPOUSE: Good at arranging the social life, but more interested in their immediate family than any extended relatives. Usually, they tend to be the head of the family. Pleasing their spouses is very important. If their spouses don't seem happy, they may become depressed or frustrated.

A LIBRA FRIEND: Friendships are usually limited in length and can end quickly. Intense relationships but friends can feel dumped without reason.

A LIBRA PARENT: Sensitive about their social standing, they want their children to look good and be the "right" child. They may be involved in planning the right course for their children (classes, activities, friends, etc.). They will carefully monitor school activities and grades, even going so far as to take credit for their child's accomplishments.

A LIBRA CHILD: Obedient but demanding, and they want to be the center of attention. A Libra child will want to be rewarded, recognized, and appreciated with love and attention. As a performer, they are a constant source of entertainment. They have creative talents.

A SCORPIO BOSS: A powerful, dominant, serious, dedicated, hard-driving boss who sets high standards. They do not accept excuses and do not like their authority being questioned.

A SCORPIO EMPLOYEE: Will get the work done if they are let alone to do so. They have their own way of doing things. They are loyal to the company and will do their best for their duty. They can get aggressive when unfairly criticized.

A SCORPIO ROMANCE: Can be both possessive and jealous. They want 100% of your attention on them. If they feel this is waning, they can become withdrawn or depressed. They feel like they give a lot, so they deserve a lot and that their spouse should feel lucky to have them. Territorial and protective, they can display concern for their loved ones.

A SCORPIO SPOUSE: Loyal, but not always faithful. They can be secretive, so typically does not share information with friends and family. They love the home and spend a lot of time there.

A SCORPIO FRIEND: Very selective about who their friends are. So if you are the friend of a Scorpio, then feel like you have been honored with being chosen. They are not very needy, so will not need constant contact, but will contact you when they want to go out for some fun. However, the friendship may be structured on their terms. A mutable sign may get along with them easier as they can "go with the flow" or changes in the mood and emotions.

A SCORPIO PARENT: Usually set up their household with very strict rules. They will be direct with their children but will have a set of chores and responsibilities the child must follow regularly. They are very proud of their children. They want them to look their best for family events, social obligations, and school. They will see their child's appearance and behavior as a reflection of their parenting skills. Since they can be a little uncompromising, it is better that only one parent in the family is a Scorpio.

A SAGITTARIUS BOSS: Big on independence, they are not always suited to being a boss. Employees may have a hard time keeping up, as the Sagittarius boss can go off in their own direction. They may not communicate clearly to their team as they are not very good at being team players.

A SAGITTARIUS EMPLOYEE: Can be dedicated and hard working, but need to be monitored closely to ensure they are staying on track.

A SAGITTARIUS ROMANCE: This relationship will be intense and passionate. They will bring out the best in their partners. As they are not good with dealing with disappointment, they may fall into depression if things aren't going well. Relaxed with a good humor, they enjoy the pleasures of life.

A SAGITTARIUS SPOUSE: Capable of struggle to balance home and career since they want to make their mark on the world. They may count on their spouses to take over a lot of the responsibilities around the home. When married to another power sign, they may benefit from having a housekeeper or help around the house.

A SAGITTARIUS FRIEND: Fun to be with, they are usually upbeat and keep their own troubles to themselves. To promote intimacy, you will have to push to discuss their feelings and situation. Since they tend to be overly optimistic, a true friend may have to talk some truth to them.

A SAGITTARIUS PARENT: Very giving and want to improve their household with beauty and devotion. So, they may be more inclined to indulge kids with pets. They enjoy parenting because of love, not because of some sense of duty or responsibility.

A SAGITTARIUS CHILD: Difficult, almost impossible to control. They love freedom and will break the rules. If they have a big personality parent, then big show-downs will happen. They thrive on challenges and love being the underdog who wins.

A CAPRICORN BOSS: As they are dominant, they want to be followed and obeyed without question. They would not like being out performed or overshadowed by an employee. They may not want to advance any further in the company, but will want to hang on to their boss status as long as possible.

A CAPRICORN EMPLOYEE: Hard working and dedicated, they are also ambitious. They will be loyal to a company only when the company's interest does not conflict with their own. The quality of their work will be very high.

A CAPRICORN ROMANCE: Typically faster at jumping into the physical side of a relationship and then focusing on getting to know the other person on a deeper level. They prefer to develop deeper relationships and will not waste time or energy on people without a future.

A CAPRICORN SPOUSE: Need to be the dominant head of the family. They must be in control of everyone around them. They may impose unrealistic expectations on their spouse. But, for the sake of harmony, they should learn to back off occasionally.

A CAPRICORN FRIEND: Will be there for their friends during times of difficulties. Being the best friend of a Capricorn can be challenging. They will only let a few people in their lives into their emotional inner circle: spouse, best friend, and maybe a few family members.

A CAPRICORN PARENT: Big on authority and control, a Capricorn parent is protective. They take their rules very seriously. In order to maintain control over their children, they may withhold demonstrations of love.

A CAPRICORN CHILD: Act like miniature adults in their childhood, with a serious demeanor. They need to be respected or they will act out. With self-assurance, they know how to get what they want and may use emotional blackmail, guilt or manipulation to get it.

An AQUARIUS BOSS: Not suited to be a boss as they are impulsive and generally disinterested in power. But, can be fun to work with as they are of a generous nature. At times, they can be impatient with a quick temper.

An AQUARIUS EMPLOYEE: Will have their own unique way of completing a task but may get stuck in a rut on how they do things. They can be rebellious so they may not take orders well. But will bring levity to a group of co-workers.

An AQUARIUS ROMANCE: Will be faithful, but that may be in jeopardy if someone more interesting comes along. If you can stimulate them and satisfy their appetites, the relationship may last long term. The boyfriend/girlfriend of an Aquarius needs to be forgiving and self-assured.

An AQUARIUS SPOUSE: Devoted to the family. Once marriage is decided on, they will commit completely. It is very important to them to feel they are needed by their spouse and family. Although they will be away from home a lot because of work, they enjoy domestic bliss. Their good moods help to enhance interactions when they are home.

An AQUARIUS FRIEND: Friendship is very important to them, but will not be a stable friendship. Contact will be sporadic and conversation will focus more on the abstract, big picture items than on exchanging feelings or sharing.

An AQUARIUS PARENT: Frequently, an Aquarius will choose not to marry or have children. If they do go the family route, they will encourage their children to grow and explore. They are not possessive or over-protective and will push their children out of the next as early as possible. Freedom is vital to them until they feel their child is in danger.

An AQUARIUS CHILD: Insistent on doing their own way and may get difficult if forced to waver from that. They have a joyful nature and they will respond well to attention and understanding from their parent.

A PISCES BOSS: Excellent at being the boss. Money-making comes easy to them and they are equally good at protecting the money-making interests and abilities of their business.

A PISCES EMPLOYEE: Adaptable and can walk into almost any position and help out. Selfless, they will sacrifice their own needs for the good of the company. However, this may lead to some long term resentment. Best working conditions are the financial reward for a good performance.

A PISCES ROMANCE: Give their all into a relationship. As a girlfriend/boyfriend, they can be demanding, seductive, possessive, and passionate.

A PISCES SPOUSE: Family oriented, they enjoy spending lots of time at home. They are dedicated to raising a family even if that means transferring that parental impulse to a step-child, adopted child, niece/nephew, or other close family members. Pets can even become like children to them. They may become overprotective.

A PISCES FRIEND: They are tuned into their friends' feelings and needs. They are sensitive and respectful of feelings. They are good in times of need. Usually, they have a close circle of friends: quality over quantity. Their door is always open to their friends in need.

A PISCES PARENT: Dedicated to the personal growth and the welfare of their children. A Pisces parent will devote most of their energy into raising their kids when their kids are at home with them. They are both proud of their children and anxious about their well being. They may be fearful at times and need to encourage their child to be independent.

A PISCES CHILD: Soft and sweet or difficult – no middle ground. Their moods may be out of sync with their feelings and the feelings of those around them. They may have a melt-down if they feel misunderstood. They are fragile and sensitive and soft and sweet (when they feel happy, accepted and loved).

Chapter 5: Birthday Charts

A birth chart, also known as an astrology or natal chart, is a map of the planet's location the exact moment of your birth. It can reveal the secrets of your unique personality and your path through life. The placement of the planets will show you the universal energy in place at the moment you were born on the planet and can provide a roadmap to better understanding your quirks, motives, interests, and journey.

A step beyond simply reading your daily horoscope, a birth chart will reveal hidden parts of yourself. This chart will show the connections between your personality and the placement of planets as each planet has a specific energy that will govern a portion of your life. Most horoscopes are based on your sun sign, but a birth chart will add in information about the placement of the moon, your rising sign, and more. This may show that you are a cusp sign, which means you may be suspended between the traits of two Signs.

To create an accurate birth chart, the exact date and time (down to the minute) of your birth will be necessary, and, if possible, the location as well. The location is important so as to determine what constellations and planets were visible in the sky at the time of birth. Two people born at the exact same time on January 30, 2017, one located in London and one in New York would have completely different birth charts.

The inner planets, sun, moon, Mercury, Venus, and Mars, directly impact our unique personalities and are specific to an individual's date/time of birth. The outer planets, Pluto, Neptune, Uranus, Saturn, and Jupiter, define your larger life themes and experiences that can be shared across generations. The outer planet significance is decided by the house they are in at the time of your birth. Houses one through six deals with routine activities; houses seven through 12 deals with matters more philosophical. Where the planet is in the house shows where we keep our energy and where our weaknesses and strengths lie.

The unique location of the planet in the house shows your Rising Sign (or ascendant). Your Rising Sign is the zodiac sign that was on the Eastern horizon when you were born. The Rising Sign makes the structure of your birth chart, showing your planetary chart ruler, the planet associated with your birth chart. Your Rising Sign also shows your external experiences – how you are perceived by others and interact with the world.

The birth chart can show your celestial name, which is your cosmic name, connecting you to the language of the universe. Your "mandala" is your own personal celestial signature and can show you what your place is in the scheme of energy surrounding everyone.

There are a number of websites online that can provide you with a free birth chart, also check locally to see if a new age shop or other resources can provide a more complete horoscope and birth chart.

Chapter 6: Astrology and the 12 Cell Salts

Cell Salt remedies were founded in the late 1880s by Dr. Schuessler who analyzed the human cells' ash residue and discovered twelve inorganic mineral salts. He then hypothesized that these twelve elements are important in balancing cellular and leath activity. These cell salt remedies have been used around the world for over 120 years. The cell salts re used in building up an individual's constitutional health since cell salts can be useful in rebuilding the tissues and organs and balancing the excess/deficiencies. The cell salts stabilizes the remedy for homeopathy when it relapses. Cell Salts are taken generally four times a day but can be used more frequently, and for a long duration of time.

Cell Salts are divided into five (5) groups.

1) Calcium group
2) Sodium group
3) Potassium group
4) Magnesium group
5) Iron group
6) Silica

<u>How to Take the Cell Salts</u>

Again, Cell Salts are suggested to be taken three (3) or four (4) times per day, at least five (5) times per week. They can be taken often as necessary in the case of acute conditions. They are taken typically by dissolving the tablets in the mouth or maintaining a liquid for 15 seconds in the mouth before swallowing the tablet to absorb it fully. Ten to fifteen minutes before and after taking the salts, eating and drinking should be avoided, except for water. There is no risk of overdosing like those off the regular mineral supplements because they are prepared homeopathically.

<u>Cell Salts by Zodiac Sign</u>

Capricorn — Calcium Phosphate

Capricorn rules part of the skeletal structure including bones, joints, knees, and teeth. Capricorns are susceptible to diseases such as bone disorders (frail bones, osteoporosis, etc.), joint disorders (arthritis, tendonitis, etc.), knee problems/injuries, teeth problems (cavities, periodontal disease, tooth decay, and stained teeth).

Considered the nutritional Cell Salt, Calcium Phosphate is a major component of our bones. This is an important remedy for development and growth. This is an excellent Cell Salt to take with typical calcium supplement, as it will enhance the absorption of the supplement. Calcium Phosphate Cell Salts will help to remedy brittle bones and can help to accelerate healing if you have a broken bone. This Cell Salt can also be used to rub onto the gums during teething to alleviate pain or given during those painful growing spurts that children sometimes experience.

- The needs for higher calcium: growth spurts, broken bones, osteoporosis, remineralization of teeth and teething in children, TMJ.
- Sore throat.
- Feeling overwhelmed.

These salts are included in foods such as beets, avocados, buttermilk carrots, cheese, beans, parsley, linseed meal, milk, and peanuts.

Aquarius — Sodium Chloride

Aquarius is represented by a water-bearer and covers the lower legs, ankles, and the circulation system. Those under the Sign of Aquarius can be prone to problems with legs (torn ligaments, pulled muscles, cramps, and weak ankles), poor circulation, and high blood pressure.

Salt water's main ingredient is Sodium Chloride. Sodium and chloride ions are important in the extracellular fluid, as they help balance fluids moving in and out of cells. It is considered a major grief remedy on the emotional level. Physically, it helps to keep the correct balance of fluids in our bodies. People with a deficiency may crave salt or have an increased in thirst, their lips may crack, and may suffer from constipation. In contrast, those with an excess may have to take diuretics and have swelling in hands/feet. This may help with instances of high blood pressure that is the result of the system being sensitive to salt levels.

- Cold sores
- Balances fluids.
- Digestion problems with heartburn.
- Remedy for emotional grief, menopause or PMS symptoms.
- Hives.
- High blood pressure.

Foods containing this salt include: almonds, apples, celery, cheese (goat and Roquefort), egg yolks, goat cheese, lentils, onions, peaches, pecans, sauerkraut, spinach, Swiss chard, and tomatoes.

Pisces— Phosphate of Iron (Ferrous Phosphate)

Pisces rules the toes, feet, liver, general physique, and immune system. Pisces are susceptible to diseases like an impaired immune system, liver disorders, edema, gout, injuries to the toes and feet, and addictions (i.e., alcoholism, drugs, gambling, food and others).

Iron Phosphate is useful in alleviating inflammation of all tissues of the body. It is the best treatment for inflammation out of the 12 Cell Salts, especially for people who are anemic. They are also the best homeopathic remedy for anemia. It is also a very good treatment for a sore throat, low blood pressure, poor circulation, and will increase oxygenation in the blood.

- Inflammation. Tablets can be crushed and applied to scrapes and cuts to help them heal.
- Fevers; cold/sore throat.
- Headache.
- Anemia.
- Increases circulation and blood oxygenation.

Foods containing this salt include beets, currants, dates, figs, grapes, lima beans, mushrooms, oranges, plums, prunes, raisins, spinach, and wheat bran.

Aries – Potassium Phosphate

As this is Zodiac's first sign, Aries oversees the head, brain, eyes, face, ears, nervous system, and the muscles. Aries is prone to migraines and other headaches, and brain disorders (mental illness, Parkinson's, Alzheimer's, etc.). Potassium Phosphate nurtures the brain and nerves. It is used to treat the side effects of emotional and physical stress or sleeplessness, headaches, exhaustion, poor memory, and irritability. This can work as nerve tonic and is great for students under stress from finals.

- Energy.
- Insomnia.
- Memory issues. Can improve attention span and learning. Great for students.
- Depression without an apparent cause.
- Anxiety and stress. Calming.

This salt is included in foods such as include buttermilk, beans, beets, avocados, parsley, linseed meal, cheese, carrots, milk, and peanuts.

Taurus – Sodium Sulfate

As the second Sign of the zodiac, Taurus rules the throat and neck area including tonsils, vocal cords, and thyroid. Those under this Sign may suffer more from diseases like strep throat, tonsillitis, hyper/hypothyroidism, goiters, or neck injuries. Taurus also governs the liver and so liver disorders such as cirrhosis, hepatitis, or jaundice should be watched for closely.

Although this Cell Salt is to aid in treating the liver, it is not limited to just helping that organ. This Cell Salt can also alleviate irritability, depression, hepatitis, asthma, arthritis, photophobia, warts, and changes to the personality after a head injury. It is similar to arnica.

- Liver support.
- Asthma.
- Nausea.
- Support for depression, gloom, fear.

Foods containing this salt include: Brussel sprouts, cabbage, cauliflower, celery, egg yolks, kohlrabi, lettuce, milk, onions, radishes, and turnips.

Gemini — Potassium Chloride

Since Gemini is always on the move, they are more prone to worries and anxiety. They govern the shoulders, arms, hands, arms, ribs, lungs, nervous system, and blood. As such, Geminis are susceptible to nervous disorders, blood disorders, lung problems (asthma, bronchitis, etc.), and headaches.

They work with intercellular fluids. They can help with sinusitis, ear infections/pain, swimmer's ear, vaginitis, and dandruff. They may help people who are traveling on a plane prevent sensitivity to pressure.

- Sinus infections.
- Sore throats.
- Mental issues: nervousness and anxiety and nervousness.
- Ear pain/pressure/infections.
- Dandruff.

This salt is contained in foods such as cheese, egg yolks, lentils, radishes, spinach, sauerkraut, asparagus, carrots, and coconuts.

Cancer — Fluoride of Lime

Cancer governs the chest, digestive tract, womb, liver, and pancreas. Cancer is weak to digestive problems (ulcers, dyspepsia, indigestion, etc.), breast problems (breast cysts/tumors, breast cancer, etc.), uterine disorders (endometriosis, uterine tumors, etc.), and liver maladies (cirrhosis, hepatitis, and jaundice).

This salt is found in the elastic fibers of the skin, connective tissues, enamel of teeth, bones, and in the blood vessels. It is used to help alleviate varicose veins, cracks in the skin, sluggish circulation, loss of elasticity, loose/sensitive teeth, delayed dentition, the relaxation of tissues and blood vessels, varicose veins, hemorrhoids, bony tumors, and the displacements of organs.

- Loss of elasticity.
- Varicose veins.
- Hemorrhoids
- Slow circulation

This salt can be found in foods such as pineapple, kelp, goat cheese, garlic, beets, asparagus, and turnips.

Leo — Phosphate of Magnesia

Leos generally have good health, but concerns begin to arise when a Leo feels neglected. This Sign rules the upper back, blood, spleen, spine, and heart. Leos are susceptible conditions like heart congestion/attacks, high blood pressure, arteriosclerosis, spinal cord injuries, eye disorders (glaucoma, conjunctivitis, etc.), blood diseases and disorders, and upper back problems.

Phosphate of Magnesium is very good for nerve pain. This Cell Salt can help with muscle cramps, back injuries, whiplash, neuralgia, TMJ, sciatica, coughing, hiccoughs, colic, toothaches, carpal tunnel syndrome, headaches, stomach cramps, Parkinson's, swimmer's ear, and more.

- Coughing (whooping cough)
- Nerve headaches.
- Carpal tunnel syndrome, TMJ.
- Anti-spasmodic; cramps, whiplash, etc.
- Will aid in magnesium absorption from supplements.

Foods containing this salt include almonds, asparagus, beechnuts, cabbage, cauliflower, cherries, figs, gooseberries, grapefruit, lemons, limes, oranges, peaches, and whole wheat.

Virgo — Potassium Sulfate

As Virgos may lean toward workaholic tendencies, they are prone to stress related illnesses. In addition, Virgo rules the lower digestive system (colon, small intestine, etc.), liver, and sympathetic nervous system. Virgos are susceptible to digestive and intestinal problems (ulcers, Crohn's, IBS, colitis, hemorrhoids, diverticulitis, etc.), and liver problems.

Potassium Sulfate is good for coughing, eczema, dandruff, ringworm, asthma, earaches, hot flashes, poison ivy/oak, stiff joints, and tiredness.

- Hot flashes.
- Stiff joints.
- Stuffy nose, colds with yellow discharge.
- Detox support.
- Psoriasis, dry scalp, oily skin.
- Constipation.
- Fatigue.

This salt is included in foods such as onions, lettuce, Brussel sprouts, cabbage, celery, cucumbers, cauliflower, and tomatoes.

Libra – Sodium Phosphate

Libra rules the kidney, bladder, adrenals, and lower back. This Sign can be prone to diseases like kidney or bladder stones, incontinence, urinary tract infections, lumbago, lower backaches, and sprains.

Sodium Phosphate is found in intracellular fluid brain cells, nerves, and blood, muscles. This substance converts lactic acid into its byproducts. It can be used to help alleviate the symptoms of inflammatory rheumatism, headaches located on the top of the head, gout, pain over and inside the eyeballs, swollen joints, high sour breath, stiffness, cholesterol, lumbago, nausea, loss of appetite and habitual constipation.
- Gout

- Inflammatory R.A.
- High cholesterol.
- Nausea/loss of appetite.
- Constipation.

Foods containing this salt include: asparagus, brown rice, buttermilk, citrus fruits/juices, cottage cheese, eggs, lentils, parsley, tomato juice, vegetable greens, and whole wheat.

Scorpio — Sulfate of Lime

Scorpio governs the excretory organs, urinary, and reproductive. Scorpios are prone to diseases of the sexual system or reproductive (prostate/ovarian cancers, uterine fibroids/cysts, STDs, infertility, impotence, sterility), intestinal-rectal problems (hemorrhoids, ulcers), and urinary tract infections.

Sulfate of lime occurs in nature as selenite or commercially known as "plaster of Paris," alabaster, and gypsum. This substance is present in liver cells and connective tissue.

- excessive sensitivity of nerves as well as cravings for fruit and acids
- frontal headaches with nausea
- pancreatic, liver and kidney disturbances
- sore throats, colds
- infection due to pus; pimples
- cellular regeneration

Foods containing this salt include: Brussel sprouts, cabbage, cauliflower, celery, egg yolks, kohlrabi, lettuce, milk, onions, radishes, and turnips.

Sagittarius — Silica

Sagittarius governs the hips, liver, pelvis, and thighs, making them prone to hip problems, lumbago, and liver diseases.

Silica affects keratin and the fibrous tissues of the body and is important in getting the minerals in the body working correctly again. It can help to alleviate weakness and improve stamina. This can help the body recover rapidly after surgery or illness. It can help ease chronic ear infections in children. It may help some people lacking with self-confidence. Silica can also be a good remedy for cysts, warts, acne, poor nail growth/cracking nails. However, Cell Salt may increase sweating.

- Scoliosis or weakness of the back.
- Improves hair, nails, skin, and connective tissue.
- Cleansing or eliminating waste.
- Lungs (asthma, shortness of breath, etc.)
- Alleviate weakness, improve stamina. Grogginess in the morning.
- Lack of self-confidence and courage.

This salt can be found in foods such as cucumber (with skins), cabbage (raw), carrots, barley, endive, gooseberries, oats, peas, rye, spinach, strawberries, shredded wheat, and whole wheat.

Chapter 7: Extra Information

Other information that may be of use when researching your sign and the meaning of all the attributes and influences that may change the horoscope you read in the paper, taking it to another level.

<u>Quality of Signs:</u>

<u>Cardinal</u>: This comes from the French for "hinge" (an item upon which something swings). Cardinal directions are North, South, East, and West. This also has to do with the changing seasons. Cardinal signs include: Aries, Cancer, Capricorn, and Libra. Cardinal Signs are characterized by trailblazers, visionaries, enterprise, or starting things. Usually, you will find someone under a Cardinal Sign in the first place, although sometimes, quite by accident. They may take the long route around, but what they find along the trip will change things for the better. But once they have started something new, they may not have enough endurance to stick around long enough to see the project completed.

- Aries and Libra are equinox signs: This means that they balance the night and day. These Signs are both times of balance or of abrupt change.
- Cancer and Capricorn are solstice signs: The solstice is the times of the longest day and longest night, indicating that these are Signs representing times of extremes.

Cardinal Signs are associated with starting things, can be forceful and aggressive, and have the drive to accomplish new things.

- Aries will initiate change with urgency and high energy. They can't wait to do what their new project is.
- Cancer is emotionally assertive.
- Libra is balanced and will consider the viewpoints of others. They use communication to motivate others into action in order to make projects happen.
- Capricorn is practical and whatever action they take will be based on practical needs.

Fixed: These Signs are unchanging and securely placed. Fixed signs include: Aquarius, Leo, Scorpio, and Taurus. Characterized by dependability, stability, and firmness, they stick with how they know how to do tasks. Leadership is their specialty if they know what the rules are, but can also take orders well and delegate responsibilities appropriately. At times, they may seem rigid. They are usually concerned with stabilizing an aspect of their lives or keeping things the same. Most change is aimed at keeping something the same (clean house, healthy body, steady job).

- Taurus does not like changes in the status of their wealth.
- Leo wants to appear impressive, keep personal power, and be creative.
- Scorpio wants to know what the emotions are of people around them and establish emotional stability.
- Aquarius seeks stability in their beliefs.

Mutable: These Signs are subject to change. Mutable signs include: Gemini, Pisces, Sagittarius, and Virgo. These signs are adaptable, always changing, experimental, but this may make them seem inconsistent. These Signs are very good at creativity.

- Geminis are focused on communication and the mind. They may allow any kind of change and adapt themselves to the environment around them.
- Virgo can be analytical and critical and may put an end to something that was thought to be true but was then revealed to be false.
- Sagittarius is a seeker of knowledge, bringing about a change from ignorance to knowledge.
- Pisces can change emotions into solidarity of all things.

Rising Signs: Rising Signs indicate the traits that you show when you are around people, the way you act. Your Sun sign reveals who you are at the core of your personality, your true character. Your Rising Sign is the sign that appears at the exact minute you were born over the eastern horizon. If you were born around sunrise, then your

Rising sign is the same as your Sun sign. The Sun indicates what part of the zodiac the Sun was in.

The Astrological Houses

The horoscope was divided into twelve segments, the twelve houses, which represent the twelve sections of life:

- The First House: ascendant, representing the self, the people and their behavior, appearance, personality, ambitions, drive, energy, priorities, vitality, and deepest desires. This House is ruled by a lively, energetic, empire-building Mars and unique Aries.
- The Second House: all financial affairs, financial independence, earned income, the desire for stability, constructive talents, values, financial obligations, material possessions, a sense of security, and self-confidence. This House is ruled by the planet of love, Venus, and finances, and stable and practical Taurus.
- The Third House: travel, communication, the mind, intellectuals, trade, the media, writing, speech, education, ideas, relatives, and academic skills. This House is ruled by logical, talkative Mercury and adaptable Gemini.
- The Fourth House: the land, home, family, wealth, ethnic pride, personal and national soul. This House is ruled by both sentimental Cancer and the nurturing Moon.
- The Fifth House: creativity, self-expression, youth, children, pleasures, romance, financial speculation, sports, games, royalty, and nobility. This House is ruled by the playful, life-affirming Sun and imaginative Leo.
- The Sixth House: public health, personal health, charities, welfare, work methods, service industries, labor unions, civil and military service, and employees. This House is ruled by intellectual, informed Mercury and careful Virgo.
- The Seventh House: agents, international relations, business partnerships, legal affairs, contracts, politics, war, disputes, marriage, divorce, and public scandal. This House is ruled by tender, sophisticated Venus and connected by Libra.
- The Eighth House: corporations, taxes, financial dealings, insurance, debts, mortgages, communes, stock markets, death, rebirth, regeneration, renewal, the occult, and transformation

of energy. This House is ruled by warlike Mars, with intense Scorpio and through a catalyst Pluto.
- The Ninth House: distant travels, foreign affairs, trade, the law, the courts, higher education, philosophy, church, and prophecy. This House is ruled by lucky Jupiter and metaphysical and academic Sagittarius.
- The Tenth House: honors, career rewards, fame, promotions, professional opportunities or status, the government, the executive and public life. This House is ruled by diligent, solemn Saturn and hard-working, intensive Capricorn.
- The Eleventh House: government finance, social programs, group co-operation, idealistic associations, theater, hope for the future, friends, and profitable inventions. This House is ruled by artistic and scientific Uranus, and peculiar Aquarius.
- The Twelfth House: dreams, intuition, instincts, karma, the subconscious mind, secrets, enemies, prisons, hospitals, monasteries, spirituality, exile, and searching for self-renewal. This House is ruled by mystical, selfless Neptune, and empathetic Pisces.

Planets

Each of the planets is used to coordinate with a zodiac sign and will influence some of the traits of that particular Sign:

- Sun: the planet of life, vitality, ego, creativity, and expression.
- Moon: linked to moods, emotions, femininity, intuition, mothers, and children.
- Mercury: full of logic, intellect, perception, thinking, and communication
- Venus: connected to romance, love, pleasure, femininity, beauty, and art.
- Mars: associated with power, aggression, drive, instincts, and masculinity.
- Jupiter: the planet of luck, religion, growth, abundance, expansion, higher learning, and travel.
- Saturn: linked with time, discipline, structure, restrictions, authority, and limitations.
- Uranus: connected to individualism, science, rebellion, revolution, eccentricity, humanitarianism, and inventions.

- Neptune: the planet of spirituality, dreams, illusion, delusions, oneness, and addictions.
- Pluto: associated with healing, transformation, alchemy, obsession, healing, life, and death.

Gemstones

- January – Capricorn – Garnet (from the Latin "granatum" which means seed); it resembles a pomegranate seed. This stone represents loyalty, trust, and friendship.
- February – Aquarius – Amethyst, as with other quartz crystals, this tone has frequently been linked to psychic abilities and can help the wearer gain spiritual focus and clarity.
- March – Pisces – both Aquamarine and Bloodstone can be linked to this month. Aquamarine is named because of its color ("aqua" meaning water). This has been associated with safe water voyages and protecting sailors. Aquamarine is also meant to produce a calming affect on the wearer. Bloodstone is connected with being both wise and brave.
- April – Aries – Diamond has long been linked to healing properties and it is believed that they can remove impurities and toxins from the wearer. Diamonds also represent innocence and purity.
- May – Taurus – Emerald which is connected to rebirth, luck, renewal, and youth.
- June – Gemini – both Pearl and Moonstone. Pearl is the only birthstone that is created naturally by a living organism and doesn't need to be polished. Pearl represents the sea and natural beauty. Moonstones are typically associated with their ability to metamorphose in appearance.
- July – Cancer – Ruby that is associated with wealth, wisdom, and love. Rubies are also used to awaken the senses and provide the wearer with a greater sense of self-awareness.
- August – Leo – Peridot with healing properties is said to ward off nightmares. It is also thought to bring the wearer great influence and power. Peridot is formed deep underground and are often brought to the surface by volcanoes.
- September – Virgo – Sapphire has been connected with protecting any wearer from harm and to bring about heavenly blessings.
- October – Libra – Opals which are a vibrant, radiant, colored stones representing versatility and diversity.
- November – Scorpio – Topaz and Citrine. Both of these stones are associated with wellness, healing, warmth, and energy.

- December – Sagittarius – Tanzanite and Turquoise. These stones are associated with protecting travelers from harm and keeping alive their taste for adventure.

Dates of the Cusps of a Sign

Zodiac cusps represent the days where one sign is rising as another sign sets. It is a propitious time to be born as these cusps are moments of surprise, concession, variation, beginnings, and endings. The cusps are set with new perspectives and possibilities and knowledge about the traits of these cusps can be truly illuminative.

- AQUARIUS/PISCES Cusp : February 16 - February 22 The Cusp of Sensitivity
    - Those on the cusp of Aquarius-Pisces are both procrastinators and goal-oriented. Although at times, their procrastination can be due to disorganization. This Sign has a lot of creative energy, emotion, and compassion, so they sometimes forget daily chores and organizing.
    - Ruled by both Uranus and Neptune, people under this Sign are very loved, brilliant, amazing, creative, and highly intelligent. Others may not "get" you, but you understand others. Your mind may work differently, but it does work beautifully.

- CAPRICORN/AQUARIUS Cusp: January 17 - January 22 The Cusp of Mystery & Imagination
    - For those born under the Capricorn-Aquarius cusp, their private life is very important to them, and they are very involved in their dreams and inner fantasies.
    - This cusp Sign might be disappointed with their real life. The dullness of reality can be constricting for the Capricorn-Aquarius. This may end up affecting relationships.
    - Capricorn-Aquarians are good at communication and their most satisfying relationships involve intellectual and lively discussions. Although the pairing of Saturn and Uranus is creative and emotional and creative, they

also admire logic and reasoning. Those under this Sign can be competitive and driven. However, combined with their creativity, this can make them a great success in work.
- Those under this Cusp Sign have many contradictions in their personalities: they need security but love freedom; enjoy learning but can be overwhelmed by life's challenges; driven to improve and change the world, but disenchanted by reality.
- Sometimes overly critical, it can alienate others.

- SAGITTARIUS/CAPRICORN Cusp : December 19 - December 25 The Cusp of Prophecy

  - People under this Cusp Sign have an uncanny sense of what is needed and are usually the ones who can deliver what is needed. This Sign is trustworthy, ambitious, and optimistic enough to make change happen.
  - With a meticulous personality, Sagittarius-Capricorn has a real knack for thorough preparation and makes for the perfect travel companion.
  - As part of a relationship, the Sagittarius-Capricorn can be a terrific partner who is dependable, loyal, and understanding. Unfortunately, they also have an intense desire to control their surroundings and may have a temper.

- SCORPIO/SAGITTARIUS Cusp : November 19 - November 24 The Cusp of Revolution

  - Scorpio has a dark and intense energy that might seem a little rebellious. But that should be expected from someone ruled by Jupiter, Mars, and Pluto.
  - Scorpio-Sagittarius learns by doing and is self-taught experts. This Sign can apply what they have learned to enjoy new adventures. This can then make them wonderful authority figures.
  - With the potential to be powerful and truly progressive, those under this sign need to maintain objectivity, not let their emotions get the better of them, and keep knee-jerk reactions to a minimum.

- Jealousy can be a weakness so people under this Sign can be possessive in relationships, but they can also be romantic, kind, and loving.
- If you are a Scorpio-Sagittarius, seriously consider self-employment. And when it comes to your professional interactions, focus on generosity and kindness.
- Although pessimism and demeaning attitude may be a dominant trait, their lust for life will make you want to go with them anywhere.

- **LIBRA/SCORPIO: October 19 - October 25 The Cusp of Drama & Criticism**
    - The people under Libra-Scorpio cusp speak the truth, no matter whom it might hurt. This trait can be useful in both personal and professional areas, but can also cause some drama if it is not delivered constructively and might come across as bossy and sarcastic.
    - In relationships, the Libra-Scorpio cusp is loyal and romantic, but may have to be reminded that jealously will not improve the relationship.
    - Determination and tenacity are handy in the professional life of a Libra-Scorpio, which can give them what they need to achieve the goals they set for themselves.

- **VIRGO/LIBRA Cusp : September 19 - September 24 The Cusp of Beauty**
    - Like Libras, Virgo-Libra cusps can be obsessed with beauty. With the addition of a good eye for details, a Virgo-Libra can be the ultimate art lover.
    - People under this cusp sign are inclined to be creative, intelligent, super charismatic, sensitive, and kind. They are drawn to beautiful art, attractive people, and more sensual pleasures. Event planning and art curator are both great career choices for the Virgo-Libra cusp. But with this, they need to ensure they aren't just focused on the outside, superficial of those around them.
    - With their sense of responsibility and fairness, they are always looking out for others using their nurturing tendencies. When involved in a relationship, they will

always take care to ensure they are doing the little things that make their lover feel special.
- Some of a Virgo-Libra's strongest points are the open-mindedness and fairness they approach team project with. As long as both sides can approach it respectfully, they even enjoy a healthy debate occasionally as well.

- LEO/VIRGO Cusp : August 19 - August 25 The Cusp of Exposure

    - For those under this cusp, fire meets the earth, passion meets meticulousness, and command meets carefulness. These traits that seemingly don't match can make the Leo-Virgo feel in a constant state of conflict.
    - The conflict may be between the sides that are introverted and extroverted. Independence, secrecy, communication and leadership are all dominated traits and a challenge is to know what and when to say things. If a person under this cusp sign has a cause they are championing, they can be wonderfully persuasive. There is an activist at the heart of every one of them. And although they may enjoy the cause, their need for secrecy and privacy may be a stumbling block and may cause problems within a group.
    - Those under this cusp sign crave intimacy but it is something that they struggle with, especially the exposure that is required for true intimacy. This may seem to be an odd struggle when, half the time, those under this sign are direct, loud, and very communicative.

- CANCER/LEO Cusp : July 19 - July 25 The Cusp of Oscillation

    - Leo is fiery while Cancer is more emotional and when combined, can cause the smallest issues to blow out of proportion. And this makes for never a dull moment.
    - The Cancer-Leo cusp is centered on movement, both physical and emotional. Constantly in flux when it comes to emotions, they may struggle for balance and might benefit from meditation or spirituality. Although

seemingly shy at first, they will warm quickly and then may gravitate to the spotlight.
- o Those under this sign may be sensitive to criticism, so be careful on the wording of any suggestions. With an an excellent memory, they can also occasionally hold a grudge. But they love to be loved and make it a lot of fun to share a moment with. Unfortunately, they are also easily wounded with harsh words.

- GEMINI/CANCER Cusp : June 19 - June 24 The Cusp of Magic
  - o Those under this sign often find themselves in the spotlight and the center of attention. But their outgoing personality may hide a collection of raw emotions, just under the surface. However, this makes them affectionate and sensitive.
  - o Although they may seem easy to read, Gemini-Cancers are known to be private about their feelings. Friends and family may not even be aware of what's going on in their life, but they will have a thorough knowledge of the thoughts and feelings of everyone around them.
  - o Once a Gemini-Cancer commits, they are in 100%, but this may take awhile. And they still may seem a little flirty, even after the commitment is made. Since they are ruled the Moon and Mercury, they want to surround themselves with people they trust. However, for this sign, trust is often hard to come by.
  - o The family is valued and important to this cusp sign and that will include friends who act like family, blood relatives, and those that have made it to the inner circle.

- TAURUS/GEMINI Cusp : May 19 - May 24 The Cusp of Energy
  - o The energy and charm of Gemini links with the diligent and tolerant Taurus. A very powerful cusp, combining modest and smart; adaptable and creative; and grounded and ambitious. But very productive, they can also spread themselves too thin at times. When you feel

like you can do it all, it may be hard to say no to anyone who asks.
- Great communicators, these people can talk to anyone about anything, but are not as skilled at listening, so they might monopolize a conversation and talking over their companions. This includes being sympathetic to friends who are going through the drama of their own and want to talk it through.
- Independence and acknowledgment for hard work are important to those under this cusp. Represented by both Mercury and Venus, they contain a boundless energy when focused, making it a positive trait, but when undirected, may cause some anxiety.

- ARIES/TAURUS Cusp : April 19 - April 24 The Cusp of Power

    - This cusp combines some of the most dominant personalities in the zodiac. Given any power, they will go straight to the top, and then some.
    - The power is buffered by a generous spirit. Governed by Venus and Mars, those under this sign are typically nurturing friends, art lovers, and thoughtful leaders. "Work hard and play hard" is their motto, but this may be a tad bit overwhelming to themselves and those around them.
    - As powerful leaders and problems solvers, the people under this cusp love to give advice. And if the advice has to do with getting a promotion or solving a difficult challenge, then definitely follow what they say. But, if you are asking about how to heal a broken heart or win back a lost love, then perhaps you are better off asking another. Aries-Taurus is not as tuned into emotions as they are in problem solving.

- PISCES/ARIES Cusp : March 19 - March 24 The Cusp of Rebirth

    - A highly successful cusp, the Pisces-Aries make unconventional but effective leaders. They're not afraid to take action, but may over-think a situation which creates doubt in their mind. This may cause projects to

idle, and then their impulsiveness may take over. This can make any ride with them exciting and challenging.
- o Those under this cusp sign will push boundaries, and may not even be aware they are doing so. Occasionally, this can lead to misunderstandings or hurt feelings, but those born under the Pisces-Aries cusp can be very good at making others feel comfortable.
- o Ruled by Mar and Neptune, this cusp is very interested not only in their own success but are very gratified in helping close friends and family to achieve success as well. They are very good at achieving this success if they can keep their impatience under control and improve their communication abilities.

Greek/Roman Gods who represent the signs:

- Aries: the Greek god Ares (Roman god Mars), who is associated with war, bloodlust, violence, hate, courage, and civil order. Sacred animals for Ares are the alligator, vulture, dogs, and venomous snakes.
- Taurus: the Greek goddess Aphrodite (Roman god Venus), who is associated with love and beauty. Sacred animal for Aphrodite is the dove.
- Gemini: the Greek god Hermes (Roman god Mercury), who is linked to deception, thieves, travelers, medicine, trade, travel, messengers, cunning wiles, diplomacy, language, writing, athletics, and animal husbandry. Hermes was a messenger god who escorts souls of the dead to Hades. Sacred animals for Hermes are the ram, tortoise, and hawk.
- Cancer: Greek goddess Artemis (Roman goddess Diana) the virgin goddess of the hunt, hunting, virginity, childbirth, wilderness, wild animals, and plague. Sacred animals for Artemis are wild boars, deer, and bears.
- Leo: Greek god Apollo (Roman god Apollo), who is connected to prophecy, arts, music, light, music, healing, plagues, poetry, truth, archery, and the Sun. Sacred animals for Apollo are swans, dolphins, deer, ravens, cicadas, hawks, crows, cows, and snakes.
- Virgo: Greek god Hermes (Roman god Mercury) who is linked to medicine, deception, thieves, travelers, messengers, language, cunning, trade, wiles, writing, diplomacy, athletics,

and animal husbandry. Mercury is the messenger god who leads souls of the dead to Hades. Sacred animals for Hermes are ram, hawk, and tortoise.
- Libra: Greek goddess Aphrodite (Roman goddess Venus) is the goddess of beauty and love. Sacred animal for Aphrodite is the dove.
- Scorpio: Greek god Hades (Roman god Pluto) who is the god of death, the underworld, and the hidden wealth of the Earth. Hades' sacred animal is an owl.
- Sagittarius: Greek god Zeus (Roman god Jupiter) who is the king of the Greek gods and oversees clouds, sky, power, air, weather, storms, thunder, law, fate, and order. According to Greek mythology, Zeus is the ruler of Mount Olympus. Zeus' sacred animals include the bull and the eagle.
- Capricorn: Greek god Chronos (Roman god Saturn) who is in charge of time. Chronos is the cruel and tempestuous force of chaos and disorder that gave birth to Zeus and all the other gods/goddesses.
- Aquarius: Greek god Uranus (Roman god Ouranos) who is associated with the sky and the original ruler of the universe.
- Pisces: Greek god Poseidon (Roman god Neptune) who is connected to storms, earthquakes, the sea, rivers, floods, droughts, and the creator of horses. Sacred animals include the dolphin and the horse.

Conclusion

Thank you for reading *Astrology*. Let's hope it was informative and able to provide you with all of the tools you need to achieve your goals for whatever they may be.

Remember, the best way to take Astrology is to focus on the positive and take advantage of them in your life! Believe what you want to believe and remember life is in your hands and Astrology is there just to help.

Finally, if you found this book useful in any way, a review on Amazon is always appreciated!

Sources and Websites:

Websites:

https://www.horoscopedates.com/zodiac-signs/
http://www.astrology-zodiac-signs.com/
https://trans4mind.com/personal_development/astrology/LearningAstrology/quadruplicities.htm
http://astrostyle.com/zodiac-signs/
https://www.astrologers.com/about/history
https://www.astrology.com/game/compatibility/zodiac-signs/love.html
https://www.lightforcenetwork.com/erwin/astrological-health-and-12-cell-salts-according-each-sign
https://lovelovething.com/cell-salts-easy-homeopathy/
http://www.brighterdayfoods.com/PDFDocs/l/LR72WHCKJQ1V9LTGKT8CGWX7TM5B1NP5.PDF
https://spiritualfindings.weebly.com/zodiac-theories.html
http://www.demianallan.com/the-best-spiritual-practices-for-the-twelve-zodiac-signs/
https://www.astrology.com/on-the-cusp
http://www.aquariuspapers.com/astrology/2008/04/the-12-cell-sal.html
https://nypost.com/2017/10/23/millennials-are-ditching-religion-for-astrology/

Aspects by Robin Antepara, Llewellyn Publications ©2006

Everyday Astrology by Gary Goldschneider, Quirk Books Philadelphia, ©2009

www.ingramcontent.com/pod-product-compliance
Lightning Source LLC
Chambersburg PA
CBHW072053290426
44110CB00014B/1666